Happy Trails

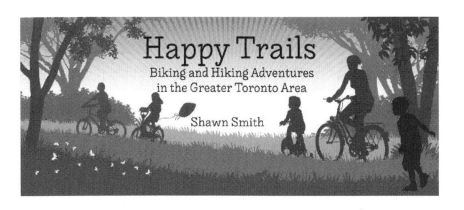

Happy Trails

Biking and Hiking Adventures
in the Greater Toronto Area

Shawn Smith

To Jen, who always knows when I need a hug, a laugh, or an ice cream sandwich, and to Noah, Benjamin, and Sabrina, who will inherit this world and make it a better place. I look forward to many more adventures together.

Acknowledgements

Many people contributed to the creation of this book. I would like to first thank Dr. John Estrella for his guidance in helping turn my idea into reality.

Thank you to Jen Smith, Sarah Peake, Stephen Peake, Jennifer Stone, Lindsay Mason, Harold Seaborn, Joey Schwartz, Marlaine Koehler, Louisa Mursell, Jen Hyland, Dave McLaughlin, Justin Jones, Walter Fischer, Michael Habib, Jason Neudorf, Zibby Petch, David Laing, and Matthew Sweet for reviewing content and providing helpful suggestions to improve this book.

Finally, thank you to the many staff and volunteers who contribute to the creation, preservation and improvement of trails and parks. You make these adventures possible.

Happy Trails: Biking and Hiking Adventures in the Greater Toronto Area

© Copyright 2021 Shawn Smith, www.happybiketrails.com

ISBN-13 978-1-9990654-2-3
ISBN-13: 978-1-9990654-0-9
Kindle/PDF: 978-1-9990654-1-6

Cover design by Luisito C. Pangilinan

"People are so often amazed at the incredible urban trails in Toronto and around the GTHA. Find out for yourself and use this great resource to guide you to new biking and hiking experiences."

—Louisa Mursell
Executive Director, Transportation Options

"I have known Shawn and his family for many years and have delighted in their love of nature and of cycling. Who better to write a guide to cycling and walking trails in and around the GTA, especially in my riding of King-Vaughan. It is a true gift to be able to share in his experience and knowledge through this informative book."

—Deb Schulte
Member of Parliament for King-Vaughan

"If life is too busy, too stressful, or too demanding, take an hour off and go walk on a trail; I promise you will start feeling better almost immediately!"

—John Taylor
Mayor, Town of Newmarket

"Pickering's waterfront trail is the shimmering jewel of our community. Nestled at the water's shore, the trail offers stunning vistas and access to the shops, cafes, and restaurants of our charming Nautical Village."

—Dave Ryan,
Mayor, City of Pickering

"From forests, wetlands, lakes and streams to the rolling hills of the Oak Ridges Moraine, there's something for everyone to discover and explore."

—Dave Barrow
Mayor, Town of Richmond Hill

"Trails allow people of all ages and abilities to experience destinations in a new way. Ajax is proud to boast over 110 km of trails, from the well-known Waterfront Trail which showcases our unique, publicly-owned waterfront, to hidden gems like Duffins Creek."

—Shaun Collier
Mayor, Town of Ajax

About the Author

Shawn Smith, *P.Eng., B.A.Sc., M.Eng.,* is a civil engineer, outdoor enthusiast, and champion for safer streets. He is passionate about trails. In his day job, he plans and designs walking and cycling facilities in the Greater Toronto Area and beyond. He has produced trail maps, led tours, and organized events that promote and celebrate the system of trails that we can access every day.

To Shawn, a bicycle represents freedom, adventure and fun. At 26, he rediscovered his childhood joy for cycling and it unlocked a whole new city. Since then, Shawn has spent many years on the trails around Toronto and believes that there is no better way to explore this beautiful city than by bike or on foot. Shawn currently lives in the City of Ottawa and can often be found biking or hiking with his wife and three kids. He has many stories from their trail adventures together and hopes that this book will inspire others to take to the trails.

Table of Contents

Treaty Acknowledgement

I would like to acknowledge that these trails are situated upon treaty lands, traditional territories of the Huron-Wendat, Anishinabek Nation, Haudenosaunee (Iroquois), Ojibway/Chippewa peoples, the Mississaugas of Scugog, Mississaugas of the New Credit, Hiawatha, Alderville First Nation and the Métis Nation. I recognize and deeply appreciate the Aboriginal peoples historic connection to this place and their enduring presence on this land.

FOREWORD

I first met Shawn a number of years ago when he was organizing a York Region Bike Summit that he invited me to be part of. He brought stakeholders and decision-makers together to create a more bike-friendly region.

Around the same time, Shawn and I began working together to create the Greenbelt Route, a provincial cycling route through beautiful, protected countryside that connects communities along the way. Shawn's knowledge and love of the area were instrumental to identifying a route through York Region. His passion for exploration and adventure made him one of the most valuable resources when it came to identifying and evaluating opportunities for cycling routes and trails.

In addition to his contributions to cycling professionally, Shawn and his family spend much of their time discovering and enjoying what Ontario has to offer families who want to cycle. It is no surprise to me that the Great Lakes Waterfront Trail in the Greater Toronto Area became an important part of this book.

For over two decades communities along the shores of the Great Lakes have been working with the Waterfront Regeneration Trust to revitalize their waterfronts by connecting them with a trail now enjoyed and loved by bikers, hikers, and joggers of all ages. The 3000 km Great Lakes Waterfront Trail is a legacy project and part of a plan to protect, connect and celebrate the earth's largest group of freshwater lakes.

I'm thrilled with the excellent job Shawn has done identifying day trips on the Great Lakes Waterfront Trail that are perfect for family cycling.

Shawn's passion for trails and our beautiful province are carried through into this book. Once again, he is serving a tremendous resource—this time reminding parents and children of the joys of exploring the Greater Toronto Area through its many off-road trails.

This book is more than a book about trails. It is a practical guide on how to use them. Eat, shop, learn, discover and relax. The suggestions are tried and true day-trip ideas, fun for the whole family. It's the perfect solution to boredom and inactivity with the kids, and it is so needed. People email and call us all the time asking where and how to begin to enjoy the trail. This guide provides an excellent answer and gives families a wonderful set of choices to begin living actively together. I encourage you to experience the freedom of slowing down and trying something new, and let this little book filled with great ideas guide you.

Marlaine Koehler
Executive Director,
Waterfront Regeneration Trust

"The most beautiful things in life are not things. They're people, and places, and memories, and pictures. They're feelings and moments and smiles and laughter."—unknown

PREFACE

This is a book for everyone who is interested in the simple pleasure of riding a bicycle. The routes, while intended for cycling, also have some shorter variations that make them suitable for hiking and running too. I've selected the most scenic and fun trails that you can take younger or inexperienced riders on. Along the way, be sure to slow down and enjoy the ride—the feelings, sights, sounds, smells and tastes of Greater Toronto await you.

In my household, when the question *"what should we do this weekend?"* inevitably comes up, an enthusiastic *"let's go biking!"* is often my response. Weeks can feel so hectic and busy that a chance to slow down for a morning trail ride and lunch out with the family brings a welcomed balance. I love the time spent being outdoors together. We stop for a picnic, run through a splash pad, and thrill in finding a geocache. We see more from the saddle of our bikes than from the seats of our car. When we take turns leading the way, my kids feel a sense of independence. Trails are fun for the whole family and a perfect playground for creating lasting memories. Years from now, when our kids are all grown up, we'll surely remember these experiences as the good old days.

Trails are the lifeblood of our communities. They take us through the seasons, connecting us to nature and each other. Trails provide opportunities for recreation, active transportation and healthy living. They make life better: walking and riding a bicycle will keep you happy and healthy, not just physically, but your mental health and well-being as well. I hope this book will inspire you to see your city in a new way and get biking and hiking for *LIFE*.

Happy Trails!

Shawn

CHAPTER 1

Resources:
happybiketrails.com/resources

"The trail is the thing, not the end of the trail. Travel too fast and you'll miss all that you are travelling for."—Louis L'Amour

I. GETTING STARTED

Using This Book

Each of the routes in this book have been categorized to help you find an adventure that best suits you:

Nature-lover: Meander down the trail and take in what nature has to offer, from a chance wildlife encounter to the sound of a babbling brook. We know how good being in nature can make us feel. Escape the city and rejuvenate.

Park-hopper: Parks and recreational areas are an essential city function that provide hubs for local communities. Use the greenspace to play, have a picnic or find a shady tree to sit under and relax.

Cultural explorer: Learn about the cultural heritage, architecture, or history of an area. Take a selfie with some public art. Take in a show or visit a museum. There are so many unique and interesting places to visit.

Foodie: Seek out new food and drink experiences. Visit a farmer's market to sample some local produce and baked goods. Try new foods and enjoy life through your taste buds.

Romantic: These trails are perfect for a casual date. Stop at a cafe, rent a canoe, or watch the sunset. Love is in the air.

Trail Routes in the Greater Toronto and Hamilton Area

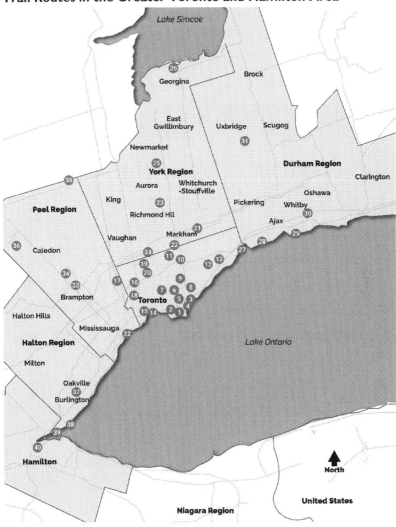

Trail Routes

1. Toronto Islands
2. Harbourfront
3. Eastern Beaches
4. Leslie Street Spit and Distillery Loop
5. Lower Don
6. The Beltline
7. Cedarvale Ravine Loop
8. Taylor Creek
9. Wilket Creek
10. East Don Parkland
11. Finch Hydro Corridor East
12. Gatineau Hydro Corridor
13. Highland Creek Loop
14. Western Parks
15. Lower Humber
16. Upper Humber
17. West Humber
18. Eglinton West
19. Finch Hydro Corridor West
20. York U to Downsview Park
21. Rouge Valley Trail
22. Markham Parks
23. Oak Ridges Corridor
24. Bartley Smith Greenway
25. Nokiidaa Trail
26. Lake Simcoe Beaches
27. Rouge to Pickering Waterfront
28. Ajax Loop
29. Ajax to Oshawa Waterfront
30. Oshawa Creek
31. Uxbridge to Lindsay
32. Mississauga Waterfront
33. Etobicoke Creek
34. Upper Etobicoke Creek
35. Caledon Trailway
36. Elora Cataract Trail
37. Bronte Creek
38. Hamilton Beach
39. Hamilton Waterfront
40. Hamilton to Brantford

Routes by Distance, Level and Type

Route	Name	Distance (km)	Difficulty Level	Nature-lover	Park-hopper	Cultural Explorer	Foodie	Romantic
1	Toronto Islands	11.0	1	•	•			•
2	Harbourfront	19.8	2			•	•	•
3	Eastern Beaches	19.4	2			•	•	•
4	Leslie Street Spit and Distillery	23.0	2	•			•	•
5	Lower Don	22.0	1	•		•	•	
6	The Beltline	18.6	1			•	•	
7	Cedarvale Ravine Loop	20.0	3	•		•	•	
8	Taylor Creek	15.2	1	•	•			
9	Wilket Creek	10.6	1	•	•			•
10	East Don Parkland	11.4	1	•	•			
11	Finch Hydro Corridor East	15.8	2		•	•		
12	Gatineau Hydro Corridor	14.2	1		•		•	
13	Highland Creek Loop	11.2	1	•	•			
14	Toronto Western Parks	22.2	1		•	•		•
15	Lower Humber	11.4	2	•				•
16	Upper Humber	37.4	2	•	•			
17	West Humber	19.4	1	•	•			
18	Eglinton West	19.6	2		•	•		
19	Finch Hydro Corridor West	25.0	2		•	•		
20	York U to Downsview Park	11.1	1		•	•	•	
21	Rouge Valley Trail	15.8	1			•	•	•
22	Markham Parks	10.8	1	•	•			
23	Oak Ridges Corridor	20.0	2	•	•			
24	Bartley Smith Greenway	24.8	2	•	•			
25	Nokiidaa Trail	37.2	3		•	•	•	
26	Lake Simcoe Beaches	28.2	2		•	•		•
27	Rouge to Pickering Waterfront	29.8	2		•	•		•
28	Ajax Loop	9.2	2		•			•
29	Ajax to Oshawa Waterfront	51.8	3		•		•	•
30	Oshawa Creek	11.0	1	•		•		
31	Uxbridge to Lindsay	89.4	3	•		•		
32	Mississauga Waterfront	23.6	2			•	•	•
33	Etobicoke Creek	41.8	3			•	•	
34	Upper Etobicoke Creek	13.6	1			•	•	
35	Tottenham to Caledon East	38.8	2	•		•		
36	Forks of the Credit to Erin	20.4	1	•				•
37	Bronte Creek	10.0	1		•	•		
38	Hamilton Beach	19.4	1			•		•
39	Hamilton Waterfront	15.6	1	•		•		•
40	Hamilton to Brantford	82.8	3	•		•		

Level of Difficulty

All rides and hikes in this book are meant to be leisurely. However, distances, terrain, and complexity vary. Go at your own pace and decide how much ground you want to cover. Getting to and from Toronto's valley trails can mean some steep hills. Walk your bike if you need to.

The selected routes range from 10 to 35 kilometres (6 to 19 miles), with a few longer rail trails added in. The routes are mostly traffic-free and follow off-road trails, multi-use paths, or quiet streets. Occasionally, short connections on busy roads are noted when no other options are available. The preference is always to take the scenic route. There's always the option to turn back at any point, and extended options or connections to other routes for those wanting to cover more ground.

Rides have been rated as follows:

- **Level 1 (All Ages)**: flat terrain, shorter distances (less than 15 km), all on trails or quiet streets and not meant to be intimidating. You could even try part of a route as a starter.

- **Level 2 (Moderate)**: may involve some notable hills or street connections or slightly longer distances (15-25 km); users should have some experience

- **Level 3 (Fit)**: may have some riding in bike lanes or mixed traffic, some loose gravel, relatively longer distances (25+ km) or more complicated directions

Riding and Hiking Time

Average riding time will vary due to factors like the type of bike, experience and physical health. On Toronto's trails, there is a speed limit of 20 km/h (12 mph). The estimated riding time in this book uses a speed of 10 km/h (6 mph). You might ride faster or slower depending on the age and experience of the riders in your group. With children, you'll need to take more frequent breaks.

The average hiking time on flat ground is estimated at 4 km/h (2.5 mph), but adjust as you determine your preferred speed. Runners can cover 10 km (6 miles) or more per hour.

Legend

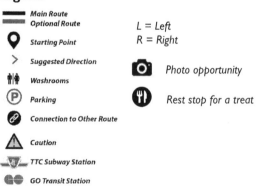

▬▬▬ Main Route	
▬▬▬ Optional Route	L = Left
● Starting Point	R = Right
› Suggested Direction	
🚻 Washrooms	📷 Photo opportunity
Ⓟ Parking	🍽 Rest stop for a treat
🔗 Connection to Other Route	
⚠ Caution	
TTC Subway Station	
GO Transit Station	

Using Mobile Apps

Mobile apps supplement the guidance provided in this book and can assist with navigation better than paper maps. You should use one for routes that you are not familiar with.

All of the routes in this book are available to download for free to your mobile phone at: happybiketrails.com/resources

The following formats are provided:

- Strava (strava.com)
- Ride With GPS (ridewithGPS.com)
- GPX download (for GPS receivers)
- Google Maps (maps.google.ca)

My favourite cycling and hiking app for navigation is **Strava**. Besides an easy-to-use interface, it allows you to connect with friends and share your adventures. It is available for free, as is Ride With GPS, and both have premium features available for a cost.

Tip: GPS-based apps will drain your phone's battery faster than normal, so be prepared for this. For longer trips, you may want to bring a portable charger or invest in a bicycle computer like the Garmin Edge 1030.

Tip: Your navigation app can work without your mobile data from your service provider. If you are worried, turn the 'mobile data' off and then use the navigation app and it should still work.

Getting Your Bike Ready

Choosing the Right Bike

To figure out what type of bike is right for you, the first consideration is to know where you'll be riding: on pavement, dirt trails or both. Rides in this book are suitable for all bikes, though road bikes are not as comfortable for leisure riding due to the forward riding position, and mountain bikes are slower due to several factors like weight, wider tires with knobs, and more shock absorption. **The most critical thing is to invest in a good bike that fits you.** It will be more comfortable, more reliable, and more joyful to ride. Here are the most common types of bicycles:

A **road** bike is light and built for speed and paved surfaces

A **mountain** bike is designed for bad roads and off-road, and can perfectly cope with rugged trails and gravel roads

A **hybrid** bike is versatile and designed to go everywhere except very rough terrain

A **cruiser**, or dutch style, bike is designed for comfort and can ride on pavement or crushed stone

There are other types such as e-bikes, folding bikes, tandems, recumbents, cargo bikes and more! Figure out your needs, and your local bicycle shop will be able to help.

Ensuring the Right Fit

Make sure that you can stand over the crossbar of your bike. When sitting, you should comfortably reach the handlebars and your leg should be straight with knee slightly bent while touching the pedal at its lowest point.

When selecting a bike for a younger person, the most important things to ensure is that the child looks and feels comfortable on the bike. Most bike manufacturers now offer decent value lightweight bikes for your child. Try to buy as light as you can.

Tip: Positioning your seat properly will help make pedalling more efficient and reduce strain on your knees.

Use this children's bicycle sizing chart as a guide:

Children's Bicycle Sizing Chart

Age	Child's Height	Wheel Diameter	Comments
2-3 years	85-100 cm	12 inches	Most come with training wheels
3-4 years	95-110 cm	14 inches	
4-5 years	110-120 cm	16 inches	Most have pedal brakes, some have front hand brakes
5-8 years	120-135 cm	20 inches	Some models have gears and hand brakes
8-11 years	135-145 cm	24 inches	Can have most of the features of adult bikes
11+ years	145+ cm	26 inches	Adult size

Source: ibike.org

Tip: For sizing, the decisive factor is the inseam length (inside leg length) of your child. It's the distance between the floor and the crotch. Knowing this measurement ensures that your child reaches the floor safely and easily with both feet.

Equipping Your Bike

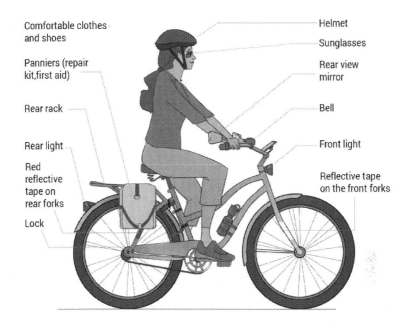

Comfortable clothes and shoes

Panniers (repair kit, first aid)

Rear rack

Rear light

Red reflective tape on rear forks

Lock

Helmet

Sunglasses

Rear view mirror

Bell

Front light

Reflective tape on the front forks

Required: Helmet (if under 18) – Front white light – Red rear light or reflector – Bell or horn – Reflective tape

Recommended: Waterbottle – Eyewear – Bike lock – ID, credit card, and spare cash – Phone

Optional: Storage (basket or bag) – Fenders – Mirror – Mobile phone mount, bike computer, or GPS – Sunscreen – Repair kit and spare tube – Cycling gloves – Bug spray – Mountable bluetooth speaker (but not too loud)

Wear what you feel comfortable in. This can be layers of light clothing that can be added or removed as needed are best in colder weather. Waterproof jackets and pants will keep you dry when it rains and from splashing mud from your rear tires.

Tip: For day trips, consider a simple seat post bag, handlebar bag, or rear rack with bag for quick access to your stuff

What to Know Before You Go

Getting There by Car

All the routes in this book are within an hour's drive of downtown Toronto, and parking options are provided. To mount your bike on your car, options include a rear clip-on rack, roof rack, or hitch-mounted rear rack. Visit a specialty store to find out what suits your needs. I went with a hitch-mounted rack even though it was a bigger investment. It carries four bikes and I can still open my trunk with the bikes loaded on.

 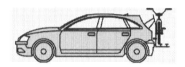

Getting There by Transit

Most tour routes in this book are transit accessible making the weekend GO Train or subway an ideal way to get to the starting point. You might consider biking one way and relaxing on the train coming back. A train ride can be part of the adventure, especially with kids.

 The Toronto Transit Commission (ttc.ca) allows bicycles on the **subway**, except during rush hour between 6:30 am and 10:00 am and 3:30 pm and 7:00 pm on weekdays.

Buses across the Greater Toronto Area have two bike racks on the front. If the racks are full or if they are more than two riders in your group, ask the driver if you can bring your bike inside the bus. GO Transit buses also have the bike racks and may also have additional cargo compartments below the bus.

GO trains (gotransit.com) are bike-friendly too. You can bring your bike aboard most of the time:

- Saturday, Sunday, and statutory holidays
- Weekdays, except during rush hour (arriving at Union between 6:30 and 9:30 am, and leaving between 3:30 and 6:30 pm)
- If you're travelling in the off-peak direction during rush hour
- Anytime if it's a foldable bicycle and it's folded up

Plan your transit trip with Triplinx, the official trip-planner for the Greater Toronto and Hamilton Area (triplinx.ca).

ABC Quick Check

Keep your ride smooth with the ABC Quick Check:

Air	✓ tires have enough air ✓ wheels spin freely and don't wobble
Brakes and **B**ars	✓ brakes are working ✓ handlebars are stable
Chain and **C**rank	✓ chain is tight and lubricated ✓ pedals spin freely ✓ crank arms, that pedals are attached to, are not wobbly
Quick	✓ quick release levers on wheels are tight
Check	✓ drop the bike from a few inches and listen for loose parts

Tip: Pumping tires up to the maximum pressure suggested on the side of the tire will make riding easier and reduce the risk of getting a flat

Canadian Automobile Association (CAA)

CAA Bike Assist offers roadside assistance for your bicycle. If you run into a problem that cannot be fixed on the spot, CAA will transport you and your bicycle to wherever you need to go. Service will be provided to cyclists where there is permitted vehicle access, and based on seasonal availability. The service is available at no extra cost as part of a CAA membership 24 hours a day, 7 days a week, 365 days a year. caasco.com

Tip: Bring a repair kit with spare tube, mini pump, tire levers, multi-tool and hand wipes. Even if you don't know how to use them, someone that does may be able to help you

Preventing Theft

Always carry a quality bicycle lock when riding and lock your bike and quick release items, like wheels and seat, to something solid.

Garage 529 is a community-powered system that allows you to quickly plug-in to a network of individuals, bike shops, community organizations, the City, and the Police if your bike goes missing. Download the free app and register your bike today. project529.com/garage

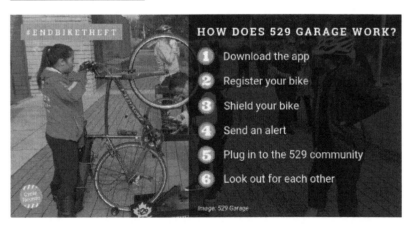

HOW DOES 529 GARAGE WORK?

1. Download the app
2. Register your bike
3. Shield your bike
4. Send an alert
5. Plug in to the 529 community
6. Look out for each other

Image: 529 Garage

Common Signs

 Cyclists are expected to share the space on the path with pedestrians

 Directs pedestrians, cyclists and other users to a specific lane of the path

 Cyclists are required to yield to pedestrians

 Cyclists are required to dismount and walk their bikes

Tip: Shift into a low, easy gear before you stop. Use low, easy gears when going up hills. Shift into lower gears before you begin to work too hard. Use higher, harder gears when you begin to bounce on the seat from pedalling too fast

Safety Tips

With proper training, bicycle riding can be a safe, healthy and fun activity for the whole family.

In Toronto, children aged 13 and under are allowed to ride on the sidewalk, but those age 14+ can be ticketed for doing so.

Be respectful

- Follow the rules of the trail or road
- Respect other people on the trail, the wildlife, and the environment

Trail Etiquette

1. Ride on the right, pass on the left

2. Don't stop on the trail (pull off to the side)

3. Communicate with others when you pass (sound bell or use voice)

4. 20 km/h maximum

5. Yield to pedestrians

6. Obey signs

Be predictable

- Ride in a predictable, straight line
- Signal your turn before you reach an intersection by using hand signals or clearly pointing

left-hand turn   *stop*   *right-hand turn*   *right-hand turn*

Be aware

- Stay alert for hazards like potholes and turning cars, and keep a buffer of space around you so you have time to react.
- Do not use headphones, text or talk on the phone while riding
- Intersections are where many collisions occur, so stay alert. Any point where the paths of two vehicles can cross is an intersection. Treat all driveways and entrances like intersections by scanning your surroundings and making eye contact with drivers. Always check over your left shoulder before passing or turning

Biking with Children

Options for Biking with Young Children

Infants (<1 year)

The primary concern is injury to their necks. Infant slign attachments are available. The start time is usually a few months after they can hold their head up. Some say that passengers on bicycles should be at least one year old.

Child seats (1-3 years)

Kids generally get too tall for child seats before they get too heavy. Seat can be at front or rear of bicycle. It can affect centre of gravity of bicycle more than a trailer.

Trailers (1-4 years)

Trailers can carry multiple children and accommodate longer trips. They are more stable than child seats but the child sits low and has a restricted view. Kids can be given toys, books, food and drink. Provides weather protection from sun and rain. Larger footprint for turns. They also provide extra storage.

Third wheels / tag alongs (3-5 years)

Your children will be right with you no matter how fast you ride, and they can participate too. Third wheels are designed to be free wheeling so a child can take a break whenever they want. Can cover longer distances.

Cargo bikes (1-9 years)

Some can carry multiple children. Also useful for picking up groceries or carrying other cargo. Gaining in popularity though are typically expensive.

Biking with kids is a great opportunity for a family to be active together. Whether children ride on their own or with you, there are some important considerations.

Many children will get the majority of their bicycle safety education from their parents. Since children perceive traffic situations differently than adults, it's important for parents to teach them the dangers of traffic. Learning happens everywhere. You can help pass on good habits to your kids that lead to a lifetime of safer and more enjoyable riding.

What happens when it starts to rain and you're an hour from home? What if there's a big uphill and your kids are tired, fighting and in tears? It may be time for Plan B. Bribes work! Take a break, offer them some encouragement and a promise of ice cream at the end. Seek a park shelter and stop for a snack. I suggest starting small and building up to longer trips. When it comes to adventures, not all things will go according to plan, and that's okay. Sometimes you learn and move on, but other times the unplanned stuff ends up being the most memorable and rewarding part.

Safety Resources
Ministry of Transportation ontario.ca/cycling
City of Toronto Cycling cycling.ca/toronto
Can-Bike Skills Training canbikecanada.ca
Toronto Cyclists Handbook cycleto.ca/handbook

CHAPTER **2**

2. DOWNTOWN TORONTO

"You have exactly one life in which to do everything you'll ever do. Act accordingly."—Colin Wright

Toronto is Canada's largest city and one of the most multicultural in the world. It's a city of vibrant neighbourhoods, each with own unique vibe, culture and mix of places to visit.

All the routes in this chapter can be accessed from Union Station, Toronto's busiest transportation hub, and there are many options to get there. The Toronto segment of the Waterfront Trail from  Balmy Beach to the Humber River is known as the Martin Goodman and is featured in Routes 2 and 3. The City's public bike sharing system, Toronto Bike Share, makes cycling more accessible with 3,750+ bikes and 360 stations across the downtown core of the city.

Resources
City of Toronto Trails toronto.ca/trails
City of Toronto Cycling cycling.ca/toronto
Waterfront Trail waterfronttrail.org
Bike Share Toronto bikesharetoronto.com
Parking: en.parkopedia.ca/parking/locations

Route 1: Toronto Islands

Ward's Island to Hanlan's Point

Distance: 5.5 km one-way; 11 km return

Riding Time: 1 hour return

Difficulty: Level 1 (All Ages)

Ride Type: Romantic; Park-Hopper; Cultural Explorer

Surface: Paved pathways; a few side trails are crushed stone

Facility Type: 30% path, 70% car-free roads

Elevation Gain/Loss: 0

Max/Min Grade: 0.3%

Starting Point & Parking: Ward Island Ferry Terminal. Parking around the ferry is expensive ($20-$30 per day on weekends) and the lots get full quickly. Take the subway or GO Train to Union Station or bike in if you can.

Hiking Options: 5.5 km one-way and return ferry trip from Hanlan's Point; Centre Island is best explored on foot

Biking Options: Algonquin Island; along the shore by Yacht Club

Connections to Other Routes: 2, 3, 4

A day trip to the Toronto Islands offers several relaxing opportunities for Toronto residents and visitors alike. Similar to a big theme park, it stretches five kilometres from Ward's Island in the east to Hanlan's Point in the west. Its traffic-free roads and tree-lined paths are best explored by bike, but are also a pleasant walk, run or rollerblade. There are plenty of attractions for a warm summer day including four beaches, a small amusement park, petting zoo, pier, hedge maze, lighthouse, and kayak, canoe and SUP rental. Pack a picnic, find a shady tree, and enjoy a panoramic view of the city without the traffic. Be prepared to make this a day trip because you won't be in a rush to leave!

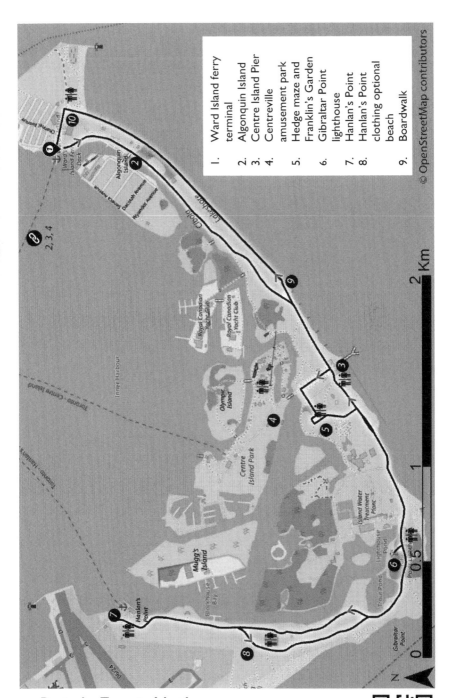

Legend:
1. Ward Island ferry terminal
2. Algonquin Island
3. Centre Island Pier
4. Centreville amusement park
5. Hedge maze and Franklin's Garden
6. Gibraltar Point lighthouse
7. Hanlan's Point
8. Hanlan's Point clothing optional beach
9. Boardwalk

© OpenStreetMap contributors

Route 1 – Toronto Islands

1. Ward's Island ferry terminal.
2. **Algonquin Island**, a residential community of quaint one-of-a-kind cottages
3. The large **Centre Island Pier** juts out almost 100 metres over Lake Ontario
4. **Centreville amusement park** is a popular attraction for kids and has more than 30 rides. There is no admission fee, but the rides cost money. Centre Island can get very busy with people walking about, so you are best to park your bikes and explore this area by foot, or take the tram. Check out Far Enough Farms, a free petting zoo.
5. At **Franklin's Garden**, kids will love playing with the seven bronze sculptures of Franklin the Turtle and his friends in the garden. There's also a turtle pond and a hide-and-seek play area, and the **William Meany hedge maze**.
6. **Gibraltar Point lighthouse** is the oldest landmark in Toronto. You won't be able to go inside, but you can learn about its mysterious history.
7. At **Hanlan's Point**, find the Babe Ruth plaque and Ned Hanlan memorial. See and hear the planes taking off at Billy Bishop Airport.
8. Stay right at the fork in the trail to get to **Hanlan's Beach**, one of two clothing optional beaches in Canada (the other is in Vancouver).
9. Stay right and go along the **boardwalk** toward Ward's Island.
10. A stop at **Island Cafe** is a perfect way to end your day on the island.

Ferry

- Jack Layton Ferry Terminal (the ferry docks) is located between Bay Street and Yonge Street on Queens Quay, a 10 minute walk south from Union Station.
- Ferry tickets ($8 return for adults) can be purchased at the terminal, but it's best to **buy tickets online**. It won't give you priority boarding, but it will save time in the initial line-up. Try to get there early on weekends or holidays to avoid the big crowds (expect long line ups from 10 am to evening). An alternative is to take a water taxi.
- Bring your bike on the Ward's Island or Hanlan's Point ferry. No bikes on the upper deck. The ferries leave frequently (about every 15-30 minutes) during peak season.

Activities

- Explore the islands by water for a couple of hours by renting a **Stand-Up Paddleboard** (torontoislandsup.com), **kayak or canoe** (paddletoronto.com).
- There is an 18-hole **disc golf course** on Ward's Island open to all players year round. No reservation is required and admission is free. Bring your own disc.
- **Geocaching** (geocaching.com) is a worldwide treasure hunt, and there are caches waiting to be found on the island
- There are several **beaches**, each with their own vibe. Ward's beach has a volleyball net and fire pit. Centre Island beach is closest to Centre Island ferry so it gets most of the families. Gibraltar Point Beach has very fine sand and a nice view. Hanlan's beach is the largest on the island and a section of it is clothing optional! Or, forge your own path and take a dip at the many secluded beaches tucked away along the shoreline.

Bike Rentals

- **Toronto Island Bicycle Rental,** near the Centre Island pier, is open on the island from May 1 to Sept 30. They also have shaded two-seater and four-seater bikes. It is first come, first serve so you may have to wait for a bike during busy times. Rentals are also available on the mainland at **Wheel Excitement**, a bike shop at 249 Queen's Quay West, and **Dream Cyclery** at 390 Queen's Quay West. Toronto Bike Share is not available on the island. Toronto Bike Share is not available on the Islands.

37

Island Cafe (across the Ward's Island ferry) is a staple for the island. Service is hot, fresh and organic, and serves up items like orange mango smoothies, quesadillas, breakfast burritos, and ice cream

Carousel Cafe (Centre Island) has a family-friendly menu and dessert bar

Toronto Island Brewing Co. (next to the Centre Island dock), formerly Toronto Island BBQ & Beer, has a vast patio. Try the mac and cheese burger paired with a cold beer brewed locally

Find the **Jack Layton statue** and **large picnic table** in Harbour Square Park next to the Ferry Terminal on the mainland

Stand on the compass on the **Centre Island pier**

The **return ferry trip** has a lovely view of the Toronto skyline, particularly at sunset

Route 2: Harbourfront
Waterfront Trail from Union Station to High Park

Distance: 19.8 km return

Riding Time: 2 hours

Difficulty: Level 2 (Moderate)

Ride Type: Cultural Explorer; Foodie; Romantic

Surface: Paved

Facility Type: 90% path, 10% on-street bike lanes (High Park)

Elevation Gain/Loss: 48 m

Max/Min Grade: 6.5%, mostly flat with a few hills in High Park

Starting Point & Parking: Take the subway or GO Train to Union Station or bike in if you can. Parking available in and around High Park, at Sunnyside Park and Ontario Place ($).

Hiking Options: -10 km (return): turn around at Ontario Place; High Park loop, particularly during cherry blossom season

Biking Options:
-11 km: take the subway back from High Park Station
-18 km (return): turn around at Sunnyside Park
-20 km: Long Branch GO to Union Station, train back

Connections to Other Routes: 1. 3. 4. 14

This tour is great for those who want to see some highlights of Toronto. The Harbourfront is home to numerous summer concerts, art exhibits and cultural festivals. Cycle west from downtown on the Waterfront Trail, including iconic Queens Quay. Enjoy parks and views of Lake Ontario and visit some sights like the Music Garden, Ontario Place, Sunnyside Pavilion, and High Park.

Activities: Check the Harbourfront Centre calendar of events; visit Roundhouse Park near the CN Tower where you'll find Steamwhistle brewery and a collection of railway trains; Fort York National Historic Site

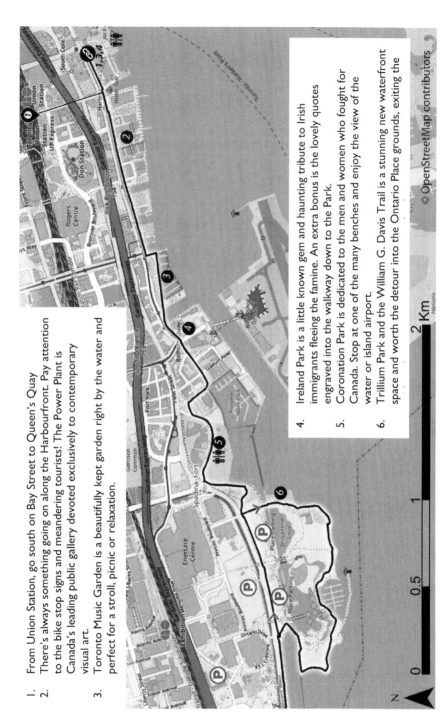

1. From Union Station, go south on Bay Street to Queen's Quay
2. There's always something going on along the Harbourfront. Pay attention to the bike stop signs and meandering tourists! The Power Plant is Canada's leading public gallery devoted exclusively to contemporary visual art.
3. Toronto Music Garden is a beautifully kept garden right by the water and perfect for a stroll, picnic or relaxation.

4. Ireland Park is a little known gem and haunting tribute to Irish immigrants fleeing the famine. An extra bonus is the lovely quotes engraved into the walkway down to the Park.
5. Coronation Park is dedicated to the men and women who fought for Canada. Stop at one of the many benches and enjoy the view of the water or island airport.
6. Trillium Park and the William G. Davis Trail is a stunning new waterfront space and worth the detour into the Ontario Place grounds, exiting the

© OpenStreetMap contributors

Route 2 – Harbourfront (1 of 2)

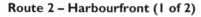

7. Sunnyside Park is home to the historic Sunnyside Pavilion. Enjoy a swim in Toronto's largest public outdoor pool or something to eat at the casual beachfront cafe.

8. Bike lanes on Colborne Lodge Drive will take you into High Park. The park has ecological importance and many trails.

9. Visit the free High Park Zoo to see a variety of animals such as bison, llamas, peacocks, reindeer, and highland cattle

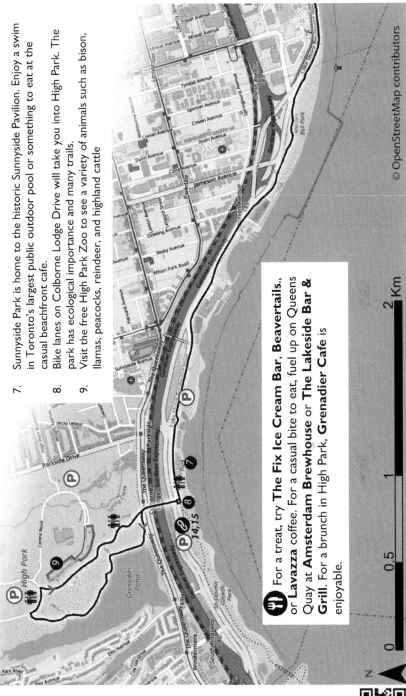

For a treat, try **The Fix Ice Cream Bar**, **Beavertails.**, or **Lavazza** coffee. For a casual bite to eat, fuel up on Queens Quay at **Amsterdam Brewhouse** or **The Lakeside Bar & Grill**. For a brunch in High Park, **Grenadier Cafe** is enjoyable.

© OpenStreetMap contributors

Route 2 – Harbourfront (2 of 2)

Route 3: Eastern Beaches

Waterfront Trail from Union Station to Balmy Beach Park

Distance: 19.4 km return

Riding Time: 2 hours

Difficulty: Level 2 (Moderate)

Ride Type: Romantic; Foodie; Cultural Explorer

Surface: Paved

Facility Type: 100% path

Elevation Gain/Loss: +1m / -5m (eastbound)

Max/Min Grade: 0.6%

Starting Point & Parking: Take the subway or GO Train to Union Station or bike in if you can. Car parking at Ashbridges Bay

Hiking Options: Make a loop to the Distillery District and take the Esplanade back past St. Lawrence Market

Biking Options: 15 km (return): turn around at Woodbine Beach

Connections to Other Routes: 1, 2, 4, 5

Activities: Volleyball, kite surfing, sailing at Woodbine Beach

Head east on the Waterfront Trail from Harbourfront Centre and you'll find several kilometres of sandy beaches, a lively boardwalk and outdoor Olympic-sized swimming pool. For music lovers, there are festivals like Jazz Fest and Blues Fest at certain times of the year. Explore the many pubs, cafes, and shops on Queen Street before heading back. Consider a stop at the Distillery District, one of the hottest attractions in Ontario, and admire the cobblestone streets and beautifully-restored buildings.

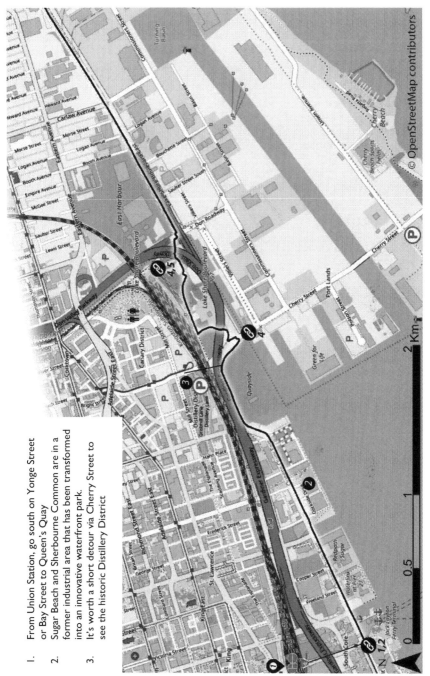

1. From Union Station, go south on Yonge Street or Bay Street to Queen's Quay
2. Sugar Beach and Sherbourne Common are in a former industrial area that has been transformed into an innovative waterfront park.
3. It's worth a short detour via Cherry Street to see the historic Distillery District

© OpenStreetMap contributors

Route 3 – Eastern Beaches (1 of 2)

47

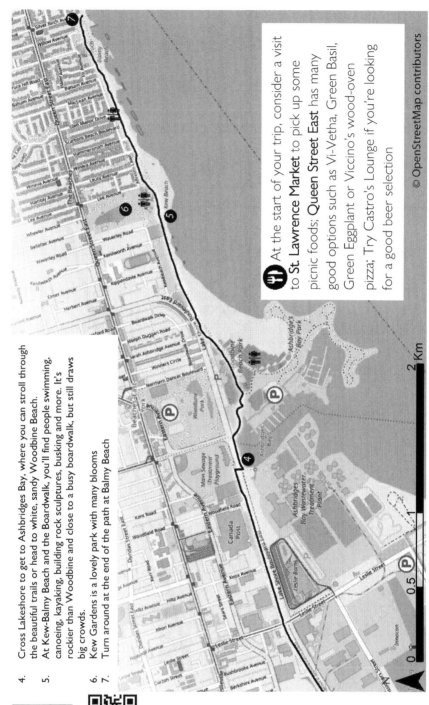

At the start of your trip, consider a visit to **St. Lawrence Market** to pick up some picnic foods; **Queen Street East** has many good options such as Vi-Vetha, Green Basil, Green Eggplant or Viccino's wood-oven pizza; Try Castro's Lounge if you're looking for a good beer selection

© OpenStreetMap contributors

4. Cross Lakeshore to get to Ashbridges Bay, where you can stroll through the beautiful trails or head to white, sandy Woodbine Beach.

5. At Kew-Balmy Beach and the Boardwalk, you'll find people swimming, canoeing, kayaking, building rock sculptures, busking and more. It's rockier than Woodbine and close to a busy boardwalk, but still draws big crowds.

6. Kew Gardens is a lovely park with many blooms

7. Turn around at the end of the path at Balmy Beach

Scan me

Essentials

Distance: 23 km loop

Riding Time: 2.5 hours

Difficulty: Level 2 (Moderate)

Ride Type: Nature-lover; Foodie; Romantic

Surface: Paved

Facility Type: 80% path, 20% quiet streets

Elevation Gain/Loss: +/- 4m

Max/Min Grade: 0.7%

Starting Point & Parking: Take the subway or GO Train to Union Station or bike in if you can. Car parking is available at Cherry Beach and the Tommy Thompson Park entrance.

Hiking Options: Explore the hiking-only side trails in the Leslie Street Spit

Biking Options: 10 km (return): Leslie Street Spit out and back from the park entrance

Connections to Other Routes: 1, 2, 3, 5

Activities: Try a Segway tour at the Distillery District; geocaching the Spit

Follow the signed route to Cherry Beach along the Waterfront Trail. You'll enter Tommy Thompson Park, also known as the Leslie Street Spit. This five kilometre car-free peninsula is a significant birding hotspot and has lagoons, coves, wetlands, ponds, a nature centre and a lighthouse with amazing view of the city. Be sure to check the park hours before you go. The loop back takes you through a vibrant park known as Corktown Common and on to the Distillery District, home to live theatre, galleries, fashion, design and jewelry boutiques, unique cafes and award-winning restaurants.

The **lighthouse** at the end of the Leslie Street Spit and view of the cityscape in the background

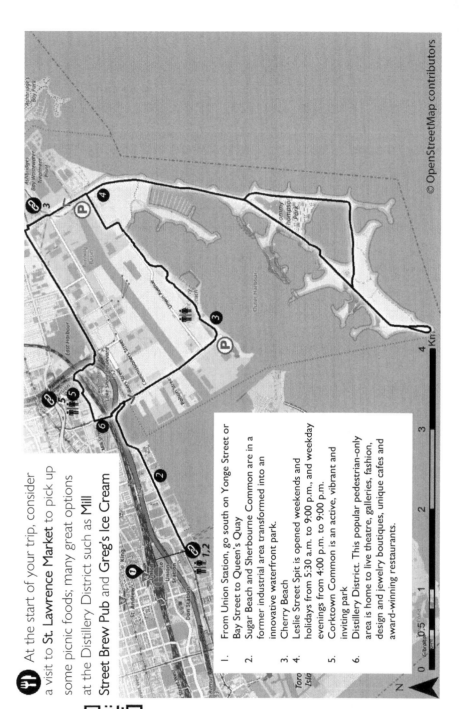

At the start of your trip, consider a visit to **St. Lawrence Market** to pick up some picnic foods; many great options at the Distillery District such as Mill Street Brew Pub and Greg's Ice Cream

1. From Union Station, go south on Yonge Street or Bay Street to Queen's Quay.
2. Sugar Beach and Sherbourne Common are in a former industrial area transformed into an innovative waterfront park.
3. Cherry Beach
4. Leslie Street Spit is opened weekends and holidays from 5:30 a.m. to 9:00 p.m., and weekday evenings from 4:00 p.m. to 9:00 p.m.
5. Corktown Common is an active, vibrant and inviting park
6. Distillery District. This popular pedestrian-only area is home to live theatre, galleries, fashion, design and jewelry boutiques, unique cafes and award-winning restaurants.

© OpenStreetMap contributors

Scan me

Route 4 – Leslie Street Spit & Distillery Loop

CHAPTER

3. EAST TORONTO

"Climb the mountains and get their good tidings. Nature's peace will flow into you as sunshine flows into trees. The winds will blow their own freshness into you, and the storms their energy, while cares will drop away from you like the leaves of autumn."—John Muir

The first seven routes in this chapter connect to the Don River, one of the two major river systems in Toronto along with the Humber. It is a key part of the trail network and  connects to many other trails and destinations. Visitors to Toronto will be pleasantly surprised by the nature trails through parklands and ravines across the city. These rivers and forests provide an important ecological function as well as provide trails for residents to appreciate nature.

Route 5: The Lower Don

E.T. Seton Park to Cherry Beach

Distance: 22.0 km return

Riding Time: 2.5 hours

Difficulty: Level I (All Ages)

Ride Type: Nature-lover; Cultural Explorer; Foodie

Surface: Paved

Facility Type: 100% path

Elevation Gain/Loss: 35 m / -51 m (southbound)

Max/Min Grade: 9.5%

Starting Point & Parking: Parking lot at E.T. Seton Park

Alternate Access Points: Cherry Beach (parking); Lakeshore Rd, Queen St and Riverdale Park bridges, Pottery Rd and Don Mills Rd

Hiking Options: The Lower Don Discovery Walk

Biking Options: Extend ride on the Waterfront Trail

Connections to Other Routes: 2, 3, 4, 8, 9, 10

Activities: Todmorden Mills Heritage Museum and Wildflower Preserve; Splash pad at Corktown Common or swimming at Cherry Beach

This tour starts at E.T. Seton Park near the forks of the Don where the East and West Rivers converge. Follow the river as you pass under graffiti-decorated bridges and through wildflower meadows. The trail ends alongside Toronto's beautiful waterfront where you can have a picnic or a dip in the Lake—perfect for a hot summer's day!

Options:

Consider taking the stairs up to the pedestrian bridge that crosses over Bayview Avenue and the Don Valley Parkway. It links to Riverdale Park East and the Old Don Jail or to Riverdale Park West, where visitors can stop at fun-filled Riverdale Farm. Also consider linking to Corktown Common and Distillery District.

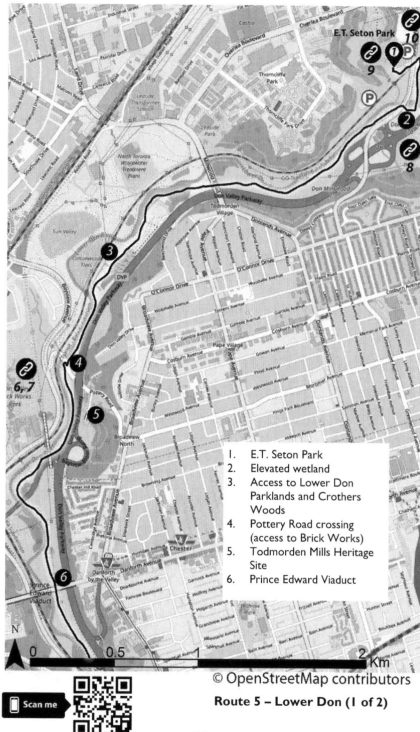

1. E.T. Seton Park
2. Elevated wetland
3. Access to Lower Don Parklands and Crothers Woods
4. Pottery Road crossing (access to Brick Works)
5. Todmorden Mills Heritage Site
6. Prince Edward Viaduct

© OpenStreetMap contributors

Route 5 – Lower Don (1 of 2)

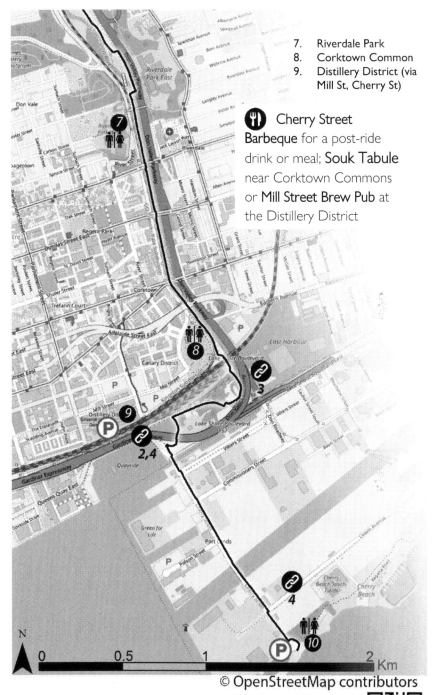

7. Riverdale Park
8. Corktown Common
9. Distillery District (via Mill St, Cherry St)

🍴 **Cherry Street Barbeque** for a post-ride drink or meal; **Souk Tabule** near Corktown Commons or **Mill Street Brew Pub** at the Distillery District

© OpenStreetMap contributors

Route 5 – Lower Don (2 of 2)

Scan me

Distance: 18.6 km return

Riding Time: 2 hours

Difficulty: Level 1 (All Ages)

Ride Type: Park-hopper; Foodie

Surface: Crushed stone

Facility Type: 90% path, 10% quiet streets, some road crossings

Elevation Gain/Loss: 96 m / -31 m (westbound)

Max/Min Grade: 8.1%

Starting Point & Parking: Evergreen Brick Works parking lot ($)

Alternate Access Points: Broadview Subway Station (free shuttle to Brick Works); Davisville Station; Eglinton West Station

Hiking Options: Explore the trails around the Brick Works or Mount Pleasant Cemetery

Biking Options: 8km loop: Mount Pleasant Cemetery through David Balfour Park along Yellow Creek

Connections to Other Routes: 5, 7, 18

Route 6: The Beltline

Moore Park Ravine and Beltline Trail from Brick Works to Caledonia Rd

Start at the Evergreen Brick Works, a former quarry that has been transformed into an environment park and education centre. Ride along a former railbed that is shady and fun! The Beltline consists of three sections: the Ravine Beltline Trail south of Mount Pleasant Cemetery through the Moore Park Ravine, the Kay Gardner Beltline Park from the Allen to Mount Pleasant Road, and the York Beltline Trail west of Allen Road. The linear park passes through the upscale neighbourhoods of Rosedale, Moore Park, Forest Hill, Chaplin Estates, and Fairbank.

At the end of one of the trails at the **Brick Works** is a beautiful
view of the Toronto Skyline

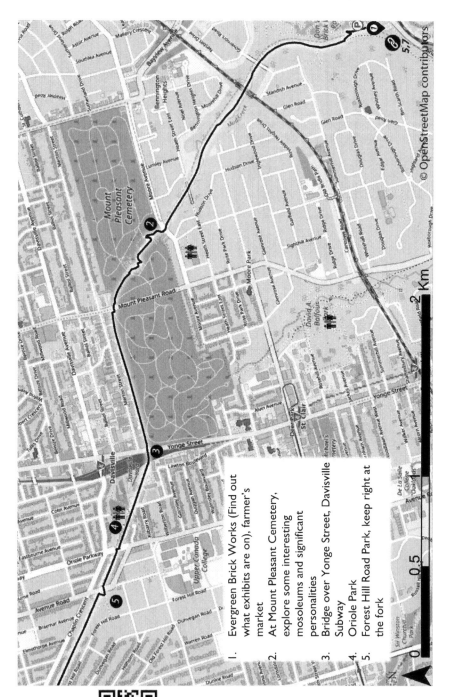

© OpenStreetMap contributors

1. Evergreen Brick Works (Find out what exhibits are on), farmer's market
2. At Mount Pleasant Cemetery, explore some interesting mosoleums and significant personalities
3. Bridge over Yonge Street, Davisville Subway
4. Oriole Park
5. Forest Hill Road Park, keep right at the fork

Route 6 – The Beltline (1 of 2)

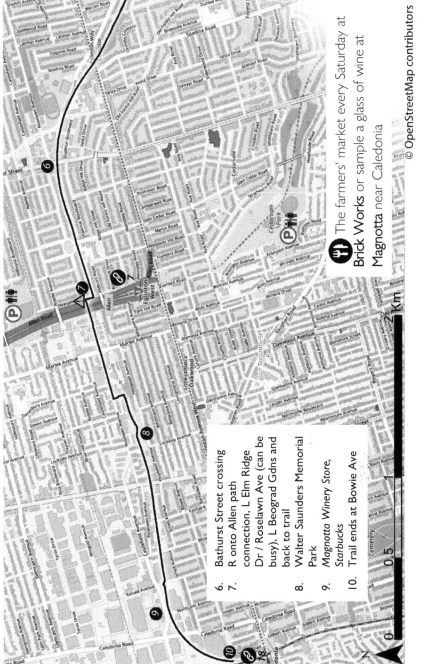

The farmers' market every Saturday at **Brick Works** or sample a glass of wine at Magnotta near Caledonia

6. Bathurst Street crossing
7. R onto Allen path connection, L Elm Ridge Dr / Roselawn Ave (can be busy), L Beograd Gdns and back to trail
8. Walter Saunders Memorial Park
9. *Magnotta Winery Store, Starbucks*
10. Trail ends at Bowie Ave

© OpenStreetMap contributors

Route 6 – The Beltline (2 of 2)

Route 7: Cedarvale Ravine Loop

Cedarvale Ravine, Rosedale Ravine, Moore Park Ravine, Beltline

Distance: 20.0 km loop

Riding Time: 2 hours

Difficulty: Level 3 (Fit)

Ride Type: Nature-lover; Cultural Explorer; Foodie

Surface: Paved on Rosedale Valley & Bayview, mostly crushed stone or dirt elsewhere

Facility Type: 75% path, 20% quiet streets; 5% busy roads (sidewalk)

Elevation Gain/Loss: 142 m

Max/Min Grade: 7.7%

Starting Point & Parking: Rosedale Subway Station; parking on side streets or Green P ($) on Pears Ave

Alternate Access Points: Subway stations: Sherbourne, Castlefrank, Davisville, Eglinton West, St. Clair West; Parking at Evergreen Brick Works ($)

Hiking Options: 7km (return) to Riverdale Farm

Hiking Options Brick Works or make a loop from the cemetery through David Balfour Park & Chorley Park

Here's an add-on to Route 6, for those seeking more adventure, that connects three ravine systems and a rail trail. Cedarvale Ravine combines wide open parkland with rugged wilderness at its edges. The greenspace is a favourite for joggers, dog walkers, and anyone looking for a dose of nature. You'll also pass by some fancy homes on a few road connections. Make a side trip to see Casa Loma, Toronto's unique castle and popular locale for shooting movies and television.

The **Glen Cedar Road pedestrian bridge** offers an excellent view of the valley and has stair access to the trail below

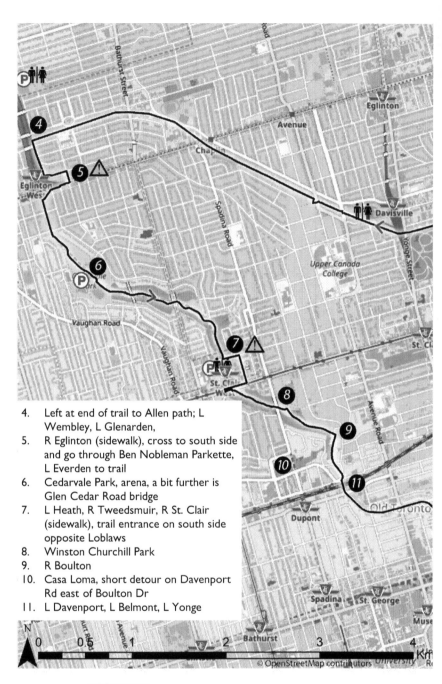

4. Left at end of trail to Allen path; L Wembley, L Glenarden,
5. R Eglinton (sidewalk), cross to south side and go through Ben Nobleman Parkette, L Everden to trail
6. Cedarvale Park, arena, a bit further is Glen Cedar Road bridge
7. L Heath, R Tweedsmuir, R St. Clair (sidewalk), trail entrance on south side opposite Loblaws
8. Winston Churchill Park
9. R Boulton
10. Casa Loma, short detour on Davenport Rd east of Boulton Dr
11. L Davenport, L Belmont, L Yonge

Scan me ▶

Route 7 – Cedarvale Ravine Loop (2 of 2)

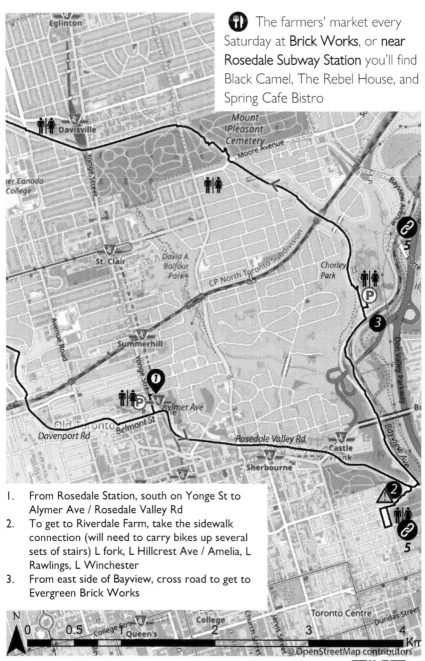

🍴 The farmers' market every Saturday at **Brick Works**, or **near Rosedale Subway Station** you'll find Black Camel, The Rebel House, and Spring Cafe Bistro

1. From Rosedale Station, south on Yonge St to Alymer Ave / Rosedale Valley Rd
2. To get to Riverdale Farm, take the sidewalk connection (will need to carry bikes up several sets of stairs) L fork, L Hillcrest Ave / Amelia, L Rawlings, L Winchester
3. From east side of Bayview, cross road to get to Evergreen Brick Works

© OpenStreetMap contributors

Route 7 – Cedarvale Ravine Loop (1 of 2)

Route 8: Taylor Creek

Gus Harris Trail through Warden Woods and Taylor Creek Trail to Don River

Distance: 15.2 km return

Riding Time: 1.5 hours

Difficulty: Level 1 (All Ages)

Ride Type: Nature-lover; Park-Hopper

Surface: Warden Woods is crushed stone; Taylor Creek is paved

Facility Type: 90% path, 5% quiet streets; 5% busy road (sidewalk)

Elevation Gain/Loss: +18 m / -63 m (westbound)

Max/Min Grade: 4.6%

Starting Point & Parking: Warden Subway Station, with pay parking available at 705 and 701 Warden

Alternate Access Points: Victoria Park Station; E.T. Seton Park parking lot

Hiking Options: 4.4 km (return): turn back at Pharmacy

Biking Options: 8.2 km (return): E.T. Seton Park to Dawes; Or follow PanAm Path east of Warden Station

Connections to Other Routes: 5, 9

Feel far away from the city with a linear exploration of Warden Woods and Taylor Creek. They are beautiful stretches of shady parkland ravine that continue from the Don Valley trail system. You'll find interesting bridges, and even more interesting concrete waterways. One is only a trickle, and two others are typically ankle deep. Can you clear them without getting wet? Beyond Dawes Rd, kids will like to stop at the duck pond to find frogs and turtles. Return the same way for a fifteen kilometre ride.

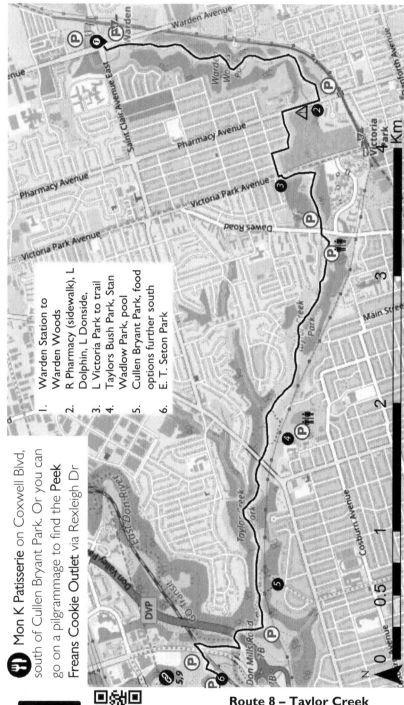

© OpenStreetMap contributors

Mon K Patisserie on Coxwell Blvd, south of Cullen Bryant Park. Or you can go on a pilgrammage to find the Peek Freans Cookie Outlet via Rexleigh Dr

1. Warden Station to Warden Woods
2. R Pharmacy (sidewalk), L Dolphin, L Donside,
3. L Victoria Park to trail
4. Taylors Bush Park, Stan Wadlow Park, pool
5. Cullen Bryant Park, food options further south
6. E. T. Seton Park

Scan me

Route 8 – Taylor Creek

Route 9: Wilket Creek

Edwards Gardens to E.T. Seton Park

Distance: 10.6 km return

Riding Time: 1 hour

Difficulty: Level 1 (All Ages)

Ride Type: Nature-lover; Park-Hopper; Romantic

Surface: Paved

Facility Type: 100% path and park roads

Elevation Gain/Loss: +7m / - 52 m (southbound)

Max/Min Grade: 6.5%

Starting Point & Parking: Parking lot at Edwards Gardens

Alternate Access Points: E.T. Seton Park, Sunnybrook Park

Hiking Options: 5.5 km (return): loop around Sunnybrook Park

Biking Options: Extend to Lower Don or Taylor Creek

Connections to Other Routes: 5, 8, 10

Activities: Toronto Botanical Gardens, Ontario Science Centre, Aga Khan Museum

A contrast to the wilderness along Wilket Creek are the manicured Edwards Gardens and Toronto Botanical Garden, one of Canada's best horticultural exhibits. Chances are you'll see a wedding there. Lock your bike and explore the beautiful floral displays by foot. Then, follow the Wilket Creek trail as it meanders through the valley to the Don River at E.T. Seton Park. Return the same way for a 10 kilometre ride, take a loop through Sunnybrook Park, or continue on to the Lower Don or Taylor Creek trails. Either way, it's a fun ride for all ages and abilities!

Edwards Gardens is perfect setting for a family photo shoot among the floral displays

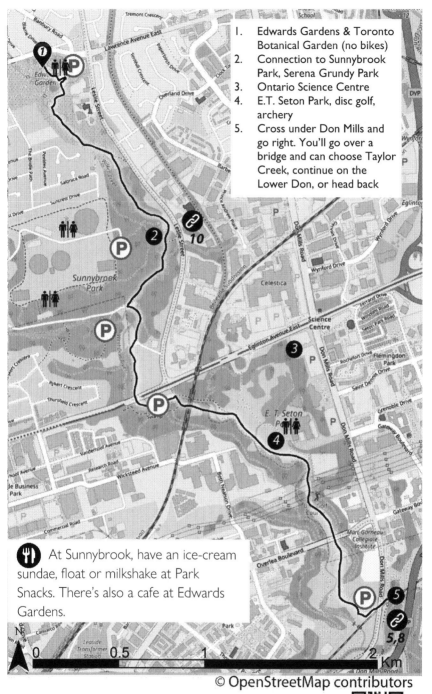

1. Edwards Gardens & Toronto Botanical Garden (no bikes)
2. Connection to Sunnybrook Park, Serena Grundy Park
3. Ontario Science Centre
4. E.T. Seton Park, disc golf, archery
5. Cross under Don Mills and go right. You'll go over a bridge and can choose Taylor Creek, continue on the Lower Don, or head back

At Sunnybrook, have an ice-cream sundae, float or milkshake at Park Snacks. There's also a cafe at Edwards Gardens.

© OpenStreetMap contributors

Route 9 – Wilket Creek

71

Route 10: East Don Parkland

Leslie Subway Station to
Leslie and Steeles

Essentials

Distance: 11.4 km return
(north route); 12.6 km return
(south route)

Riding Time: 1 hour

Difficulty: Level 1 (All Ages)

Ride Type: Nature-lover;
Park-Hopper

Surface: Paved

Facility Type: 100% path

Elevation Gain/Loss:
+30 m / -13 m (northbound)

Max/Min Grade: 3.8%

Starting Point & Parking:
Leslie Subway Station; parking
available in northwest corner of
Sheppard and Leslie, off of Old
Leslie St.

Alternate Access Points:
Leslie St north of Steeles Ave;
Cummer GO Station, Cummer
Park Community Centre,
Edwards Gardens

Hiking Options: Off-shoot to
Bestview Park from Cummer
Avenue

Biking Options: Go north or
south from Leslie Station

**Connections to Other
Routes**: 5, 9, 11, 22

Explore the linear
greenway that is the East
Don Parkland. It's safe and
fun for all levels as well as
runners and hikers. In the
Fall, you can see salmon
swimming upstream to
spawn. Start at Leslie
Station and choose your
own adventure.

If you go north to Steeles,
you can turn around for an
11 kilometre ride, continue
north into York Region on
the Lake to Lake Route,
east on Duncan Creek
Trail, or west on the Finch
Hydro Corridor trail. If you
go south, you can stop at
Edwards Gardens or
continue along Wilket
Creek from there. There
are many options!

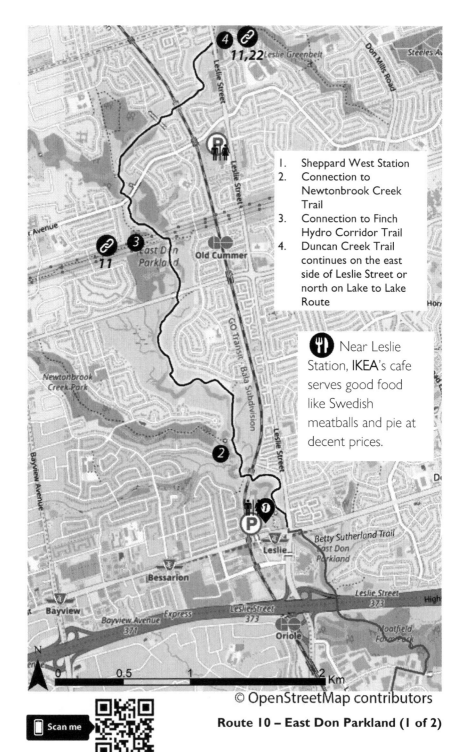

1. Sheppard West Station
2. Connection to Newtonbrook Creek Trail
3. Connection to Finch Hydro Corridor Trail
4. Duncan Creek Trail continues on the east side of Leslie Street or north on Lake to Lake Route

🍴 Near Leslie Station, **IKEA**'s cafe serves good food like Swedish meatballs and pie at decent prices.

© OpenStreetMap contributors

Route 10 – East Don Parkland (1 of 2)

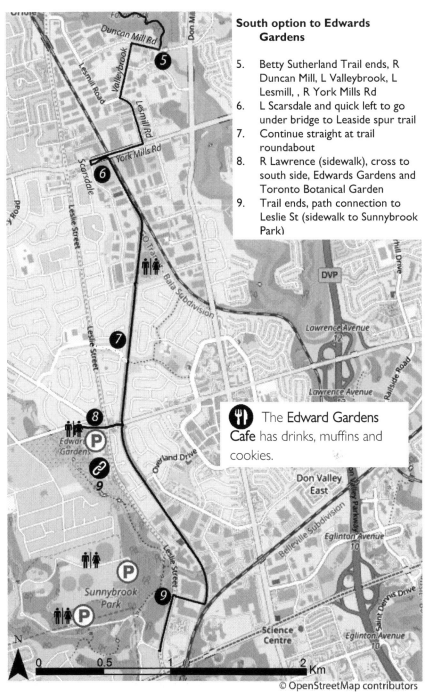

South option to Edwards Gardens

5. Betty Sutherland Trail ends, R Duncan Mill, L Valleybrook, L Lesmill, , R York Mills Rd
6. L Scarsdale and quick left to go under bridge to Leaside spur trail
7. Continue straight at trail roundabout
8. R Lawrence (sidewalk), cross to south side, Edwards Gardens and Toronto Botanical Garden
9. Trail ends, path connection to Leslie St (sidewalk to Sunnybrook Park)

The Edward Gardens Cafe has drinks, muffins and cookies.

© OpenStreetMap contributors

Route 10 – East Don Parkland (2 of 2)

Route 11: Finch Hydro Corridor East

Yonge Street to East Don Parklands to Duncan Creek Trail

Distance: 15.8 km return

Riding Time: 1.5 hours

Difficulty: Level 2 (Moderate)

Ride Type: Park-Hopper; Cultural Explorer

Surface: Paved, short segment of crushed stone along Duncan Creek

Facility Type: 95% path, 5% quiet streets

Elevation Gain/Loss: +47m / -49m (eastbound)

Max/Min Grade: 7.2%

Starting Point & Parking: Finch Subway Station ($)

Alternate Access Points: McNicoll Park and many other access points

Hiking Options: 7 km (return): Cummer Park Community Centre to McNicoll Park, access trail via Cummer and north on Pineway

Biking Options: Connect with the Lake to Lake Route north of Steeles or south on the East Don Parklands

Connections to Other Routes: 10, 19, 22

Start at Finch Subway Station and head east along the Finch Hydro Corridor recreational trail. As you descend to the Don River, you'll come to a hill offering a great view of the corridor. The trail switches back and forth across the slope. Connect to the East Don Parkland Trail and on to the Duncan Creek Trail. You'll cross a bridge at German Mills Creek and end at a park where you can picnic or cool off in the splash pad. Turn around at McNicoll Park and end with a treat from Pastel Creperie & Dessert House on Yonge Street.

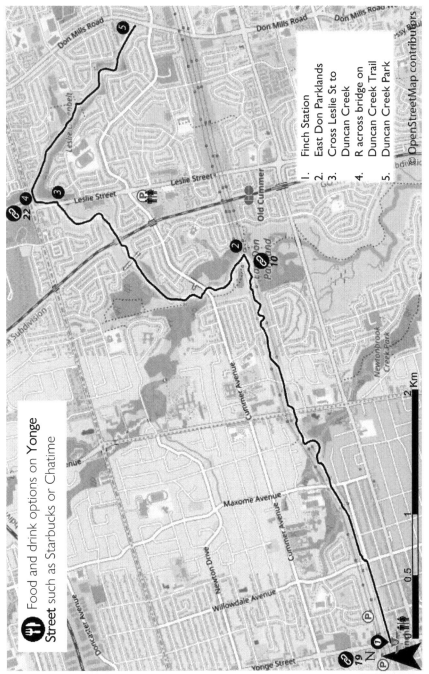

Food and drink options on Yonge Street such as Starbucks or Chatime

1. Finch Station
2. East Don Parklands
3. Cross Leslie St to Duncan Creek
4. R across bridge on Duncan Creek Trail
5. Duncan Creek Park

© OpenStreetMap contributors

Route 11 – Finch Hydro Corridor East

Scan me

Route 12: Gatineau Hydro Corridor Loop

Thomson Memorial Park to Scarborough Golf Club Road to West Highland Creek

Distance: 14.2 km loop

Riding Time: 1.5 hours

Difficulty: Level 1 (All Ages)

Ride Type: Park-Hopper; Cultural Explorer

Surface: Paved

Facility Type: 70% path, 27% quiet streets, 3% busy roads (sidewalk)

Elevation Gain/Loss: 56 m

Max/Min Grade: +5.5% / -7.4%

Starting Point & Parking: Parking lot at Thomson Memorial Park

Hiking Options: Loop around Thomson Memorial Park

Biking Options: 8.2 km (return): turn around at Scarborough Golf Club Rd

Connections to Other Routes: 13, PanAm Path

This tour begins at Thomson Memorial Park, one of the nicest in Scarborough, where you can visit a historic house. Follow the Gatineau Hydro Corridor trail and connect with the Highland Creek Trail and some quiet streets for a 14 km loop. Cool off in the splash pad and have a picnic upon your return.

Best rest stop for a treat:

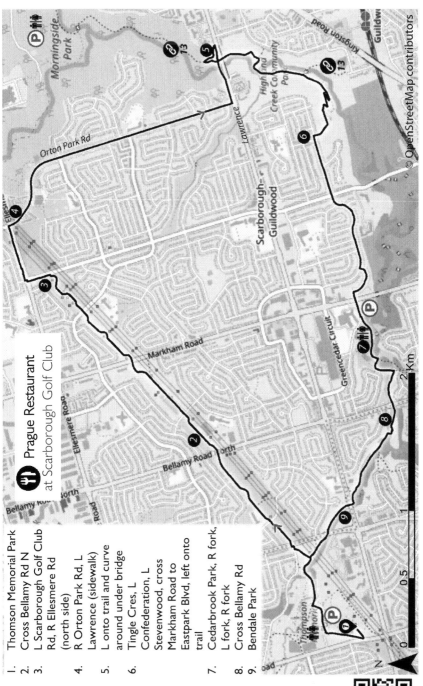

1. Thomson Memorial Park
2. Cross Bellamy Rd N
3. L Scarborough Golf Club Rd, R Ellesmere Rd (north side)
4. R Orton Park Rd, L Lawrence (sidewalk)
5. L onto trail and curve around under bridge
6. Tingle Cres, L Confederation, L Stevenwood, cross Markham Road to Eastpark Blvd, left onto trail
7. Cedarbrook Park, R fork, L fork, R fork
8. Cross Bellamy Rd
9. Bendale Park

Prague Restaurant
at Scarborough Golf Club

© OpenStreetMap contributors

Route 12 – Gatineau Hydro Corridor Loop

Scan me

81

Route 13: Highland Creek

Rouge Hill to Guildwood Village

Distance: 11.2 km one-way, return on GO Train; or 19.0 km loop

Riding Time: 1.5 hours

Difficulty: Level 1 (All Ages)

Ride Type: Nature-lover; Park-Hopper

Surface: Paved

Facility Type: 98% path; 2% quiet streets

Elevation Gain/Loss: +72 m / -14 m (westbound)

Max/Min Grade: 6.1%

Starting Point & Parking: Rouge Hill GO parking lot

Alternate Access Points: Guildwood GO parking lot; Morningside Park

Hiking Options: You could start at Morningside Park and do an out and back in either direction. Or, hike the 4 km return from Rouge Hill to Port Union.

Biking Options: 17km loop option using Waterfront Trail with some on-road segments

Connections to Other

Highland Creek is the best river trail in the Scarborough area of Toronto, emptying into Lake Ontario at the eastern end of the Scarborough Bluffs. The paved trail takes you through wooded areas along the river. Start at Rouge Hill GO Station, steps from the Waterfront Trail, and follow the continuous off-road route where you can stop, relax in nature, and enjoy the views. Take the GO Train back from Guildwood, or make it a loop with some on-road segments close to the shoreline.

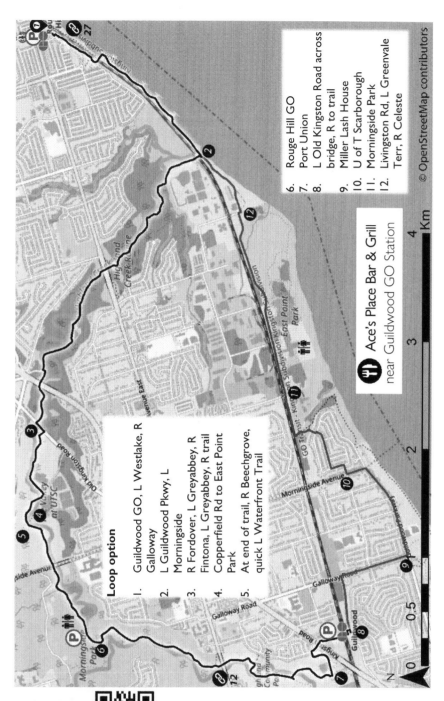

Loop option

1. Guildwood GO, L Westlake, R Galloway
2. L Guildwood Pkwy, L Morningside
3. R Fordover, L Greyabbey, R Fintona, L Greyabbey, R trail
4. Copperfield Rd to East Point Park
5. At end of trail, R Beechgrove, quick L Waterfront Trail
6. Rouge Hill GO
7. Port Union
8. L Old Kingston Road across bridge, R to trail
9. Miller Lash House
10. U of T Scarborough
11. Morningside Park
12. Livingston Rd, L Greenvale Terr, R Celeste

🍴 **Ace's Place Bar & Grill** near Guildwood GO Station

© OpenStreetMap contributors

N

Km
0   0.5   1   2   3   4

Scan me

Route 13 – Highland Creek Loop

CHAPTER **4**

4. WEST TORONTO

"Twenty years from now, you will be more disappointed by the things you didn't do than the ones you did. So throw off the bowlines. Sail away from the safe harbour. Catch the trade winds in your sails. Explore. Dream. Discover."—Mark Twain

The first five routes in this chapter are within the Humber River watershed, the largest watershed and longest trail system in Toronto. The Humber was used by First Nations people as a trade route between Lake Ontario and the Upper Great Lakes to the north. In 1999, it was designated a Canadian Heritage River to recognize its historical significance. It is also an important corridor for fish, migratory songbirds and monarch butterflies.

Waterfront Trail from
Marie Curis Park to
Sunnyside Park

Distance: 22.2 km return

Riding Time: 2.5 hours

Difficulty: Level 1 (All Ages)

Ride Type: Park-Hopper;
Cultural Explorer; Romantic

Surface: Paved

Facility Type: 66% path, 23%
quiet streets, 11% bike lane

Elevation Gain/Loss: +/- 2 m

Max/Min Grade:
+1.1% / -1.3% (westbound)

Starting Point & Parking:
Parking at Marie Curtis Park or
Long Branch GO Station (trail
at Maurice J. Breen Park)

Alternate Access Points:
Parking at Colonel Samuel
Smith Park, Humber Bay Park,
Sunnyside Park

Hiking Options: 6km return:
Marie Curtis Park to Colonel
Samuel Smith Park

Biking Options: 20km return:
turn around at Humber Bridge;
20km: bike to Union Station
and take the train back to Long
Branch GO Station

**Connections to Other
Routes:** 2, 15, 32

Cruise along the
Waterfront Trail and take
in the greenery and
panaromic lake views. Pass
over the iconic Humber
Bay Arch Bridge at the
mouth of the Humber
River. Opportunities for a
picnic include Humber Bay
Park, Colonel Samuel
Smith Park and Marie
Curtis Park. While there,
delight in the water birds,
watch all the people out
for a stroll or just relax
under a shady tree. At
Sunnyside, have an ice
cream from the snack
shop and a cool dip in the
lake or pool before
heading back.

Humber Bay Arch Bridge or view of the Toronto skyline at nearby **Sheldon lookout**

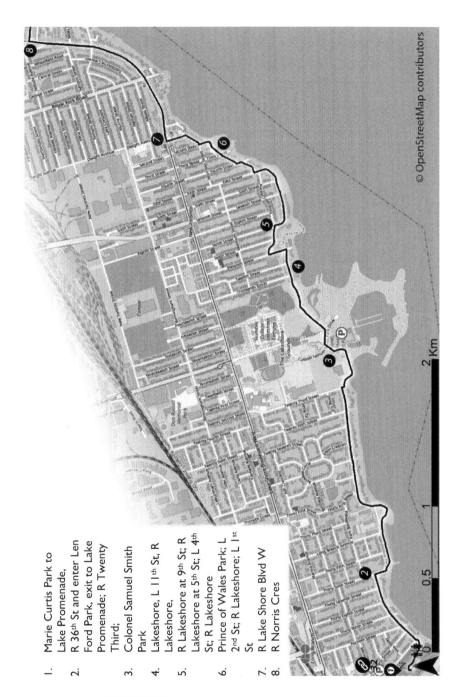

© OpenStreetMap contributors

1. Marie Curtis Park to Lake Promenade,
2. R 36th St and enter Len Ford Park, exit to Lake Promenade; R Twenty Third;
3. Colonel Samuel Smith Park
4. Lakeshore, L 11th St, R Lakeshore,
5. R Lakeshore at 9th St; R Lakeshore at 5th St; L 4th St; R Lakeshore
6. Prince of Wales Park; L 2nd St; R Lakeshore; L 1st St
7. R Lake Shore Blvd W
8. R Norris Cres

Route 14 – Western Parks (1 of 2)

9. Humber Bay Park West
10. Humber Bay Arch Bridge
11. Sunnyside Park

🍴 Sunnyside Pavilion Cafe; Firkin on the Bay; Bicycle Cafe at Amos Waites Park

N

| 0 | 0.5 | 1 | 2 Km |

Route 14 – Western Parks (2 of 2)

Scan me

Route 15: Lower Humber

Old Mill Station to Waterfront Trail and Sunnyside Park

Distance: 11.4 km return

Riding Time: 1.5 hours

Difficulty: Level 2 (Moderate)

Ride Type: Nature-lover; Romantic

Surface: Paved

Facility Type: 80% path, 20% quiet streets

Elevation Gain/Loss: +23 m / -30 m (southbound)

Max/Min Grade: 5.8%

Starting Point & Parking: Old Mill Subway Station, parking east of the station at Hurricane Hazel Memorial or Etienne Brule Park

Alternate Access Points: King's Mill Park, Sunnyside Park

Hiking Options: Follow the Discovery Walk signage to make a loop using both sides of the river

Biking Options: 15 km to Union Station and take subway back; High Park using bike lanes on Colborne Lodge Rd

Connections to Other Routes: 2, 14, 16

For a short and sweet ride or walk, start at the Old Mill Subway Station and head south on the Humber Trail and a few quiet street connections. At certain times of the year, you can see salmon swimming upstream to spawn. At the mouth of the mighty Humber, cross the iconic arch bridge to Sunnyside Park where you can enjoy the beach, pool, and cafe before heading back, or continue on the Waterfront Trail if you're feeling like more.

Activity: Canoe, kayak and SUP rental, lessons and guided tours are available (torontoadventures.ca)

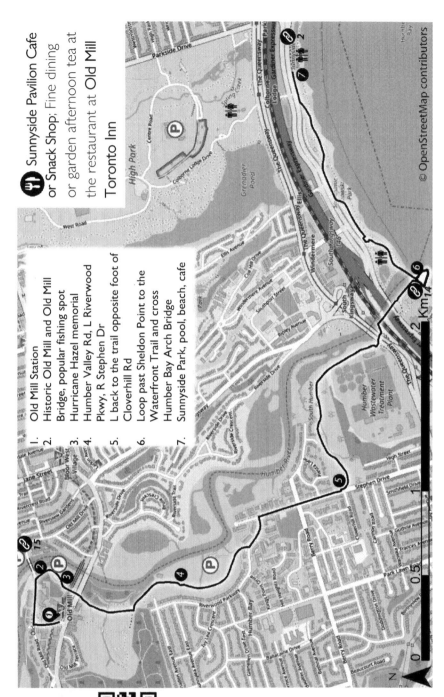

Sunnyside Pavilion Cafe or Snack Shop; Fine dining or garden afternoon tea at the restaurant at Old Mill Toronto Inn

1. Old Mill Station
2. Historic Old Mill and Old Mill Bridge, popular fishing spot
3. Hurricane Hazel memorial
4. Humber Valley Rd, L Riverwood Pkwy, R Stephen Dr
5. L back to the trail opposite foot of Cloverhill Rd
6. Loop past Sheldon Point to the Waterfront Trail and cross Humber Bay Arch Bridge
7. Sunnyside Park, pool, beach, cafe

© OpenStreetMap contributors

Scan me

Route 15 – Lower Humber

Route 16: Upper Humber

South of Steeles Avenue to
Old Mill Subway Station

Essentials

Distance: 37.4 km return

Riding Time: 3.5 hours

Difficulty: Level 2 (Moderate)

Ride Type: Park-Hopper;
Nature-lover

Surface: Paved

Facility Type: 95% path, 5%
busy road (sidewalk)

Elevation Gain/Loss: +50 m /
-100 m (southbound)

Max/Min Grade: 8.5%

Starting Point & Parking:
Parking at Rountree Mills Park
(access off of Islington)

Alternate Access Points:
Thackeray Park, Bluehaven
Park, Summerlea Park, Pine
Point Park, Old Mill Station

Hiking Options: 8.5 km
(return): to West Humber Trail

Biking Options:
-15 km loop via West Humber
Trail and Silverstone Dr
-17 km: turn around at Weston
Rd
-34 km to Union Station,
return to Weston UP Express

**Connections to Other
Routes:** 15, 17, 18

Descend into the valley and
be taken to another world.
This is an easy ride along the
river that the whole family
can enjoy. Go as far as you
like and turn back, or if
you're feeling energetic,
continue to the Lower
Humber (Route 15) all the
way to the Waterfront.
You'll have many scenic
views as the trail crosses
from one side of the river to
the other. Stop at one of the
parks along the way and
spend a good chunk of time
in the great outdoors.

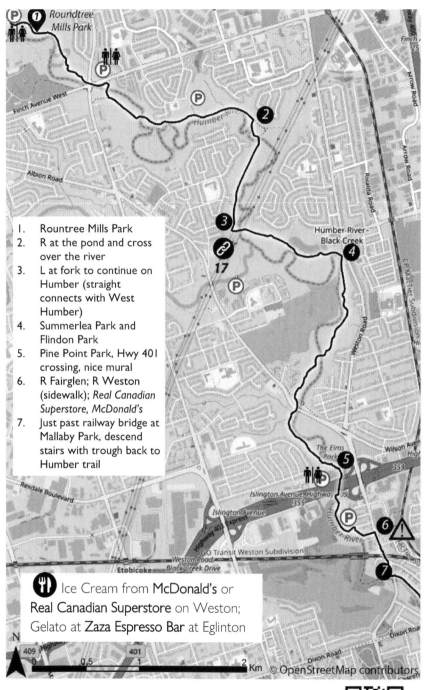

1. Rountree Mills Park
2. R at the pond and cross over the river
3. L at fork to continue on Humber (straight connects with West Humber)
4. Summerlea Park and Flindon Park
5. Pine Point Park, Hwy 401 crossing, nice mural
6. R Fairglen; R Weston (sidewalk); *Real Canadian Superstore, McDonald's*
7. Just past railway bridge at Mallaby Park, descend stairs with trough back to Humber trail

Ice Cream from **McDonald's** or **Real Canadian Superstore** on Weston; Gelato at **Zaza Espresso Bar** at Eglinton

Route 16 – Upper Humber (1 of 2)

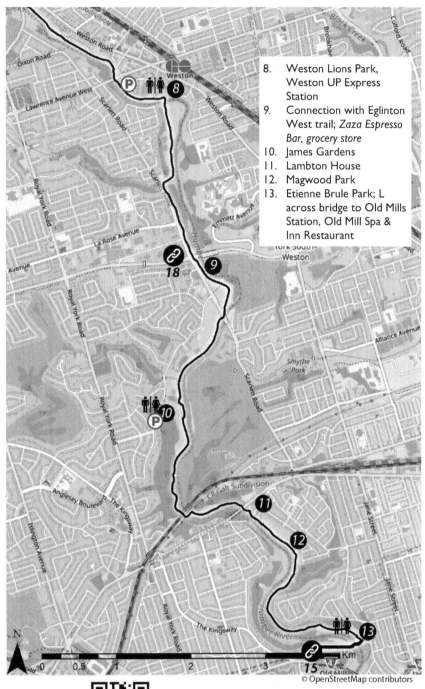

8. Weston Lions Park, Weston UP Express Station
9. Connection with Eglinton West trail; *Zaza Espresso Bar, grocery store*
10. James Gardens
11. Lambton House
12. Magwood Park
13. Etienne Brule Park; L across bridge to Old Mills Station, Old Mill Spa & Inn Restaurant

© OpenStreetMap contributors

Route 16 – Upper Humber (2 of 2)

Route 17: West Humber

Indian Line Campground to Summerlea Park and Humber Trail

Essentials

Distance: 19.4 km return

Riding Time: 2 hours

Difficulty: Level 1 (All Ages)

Ride Type: Park-Hopper; Nature lover

Surface: Paved

Facility Type: 100% path

Elevation Gain/Loss: +12m / -47 m (eastbound)

Max/Min Grade: 6.4%

Starting Point & Parking: Parking at Indian Line Campground ($) or Humberwood Community Centre

Alternate Access Points: Humber Arboretum, Summerlea Park

Hiking Options: 8 km (return) to Humber Arborteum

Biking Options: Continue on Humber Trail

Connections to Other Routes: 16

Start your outdoor adventure at Indian Line, the closest campground to downtown Toronto, and follow the West branch of the Humber River Trail. You will see the Claireville Reservoir Dam as well as Humber College Arboretum where you can explore the gardens. Picnic at Summerlea Park before returning back, or continue on the main Humber Trail north or south. Either way, you will see a lot of greenery on one of the best trail systems in the city.

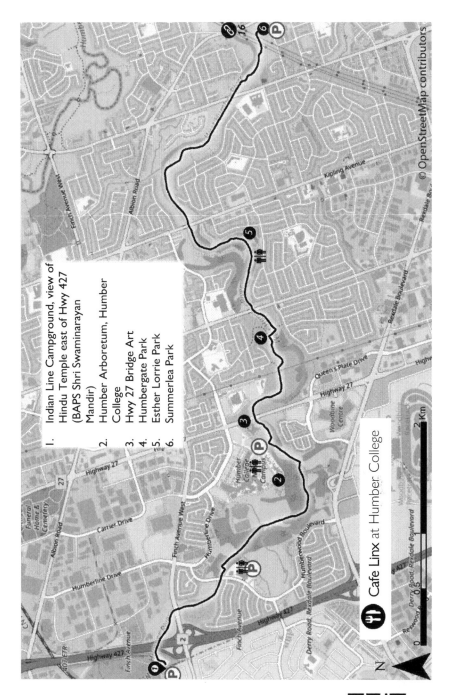

1. Indian Line Campground, view of Hindu Temple east of Hwy 427 (BAPS Shri Swaminarayan Mandir)
2. Humber Arboretum, Humber College
3. Hwy 27 Bridge Art
4. Humbergate Park
5. Esther Lorrie Park
6. Summerlea Park

Cafe Linx at Humber College

Route 17 – West Humber

Scan me

Route 18: Eglinton West

Centennial Park to Scarlett Mills and Humber Trail

Essentials

Distance: 19.6 km return

Riding Time: 2 hours

Difficulty: Level 2 (Moderate)

Ride Type: Park-hopper; Cultural Explorer

Surface: Paved

Facility Type: 95% path, 5% quiet streets

Elevation Gain/Loss: +5 m / -51 m (eastbound)

Max/Min Grade: 4.5%

Starting Point: Parking at Centennial Park

Alternate Access Points: Renforth MiWay LRT Station

Hiking Options: Explore the trails in Centennial Park

Biking Options: Continue on the Humber Trail

Connections to Other Routes: 6, 16, 33

Start at Centennial Park, the park with everything: mini-putt, go karting, field sports, volleyball, indoor swimming pool, fishing, greenhouse, gardens, disc golf and more. Follow the Eglinton West path as it descends to the Humber River. At Scarlett Mills Golf Course, have lunch, drinks or snacks at the restaurant. You can ride back, take the bus or continue north or south on the Humber Trail for more.

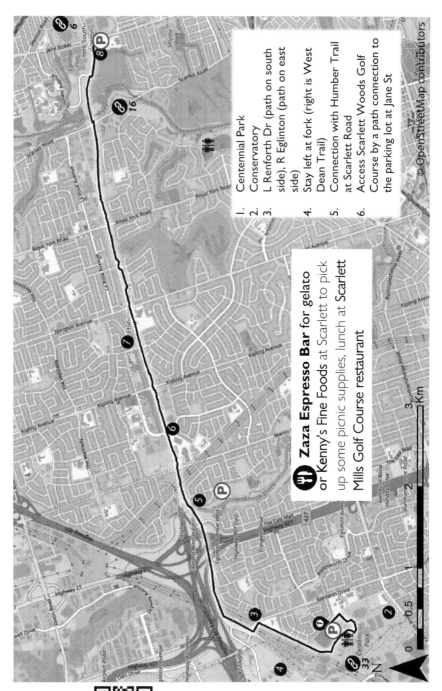

1. Centennial Park Conservatory
2. L Renforth Dr (path on south side), R Eglinton (path on east side)
3. Stay left at fork (right is West Dean Trail)
4. Connection with Humber Trail at Scarlett Road
5. Access Scarlett Woods Golf Course at Scarlett Road
6. Course by a path connection to the parking lot at Jane St

🍴 **Zaza Espresso Bar** for gelato or Kenny's Fine Foods at Scarlett to pick up some picnic supplies, lunch at **Scarlett Mills Golf Course restaurant**

©OpenStreetMap contributors

Route 18 – Eglinton West

Scan me

Essentials

Distance: 25.0 km return

Riding Time: 2.5 hours

Difficulty: Level 2 (Moderate)

Ride Type: Park-Hopper; Cultural Explorer

Surface: Paved

Facility Type: 90% path, 10% quiet streets

Elevation Gain/Loss: +34 m / -49 m (eastbound)

Max/Min Grade: 4.3%

Starting Point & Parking: Pay Parking at Pioneer Village Subway Station, Black Creek Pioneer Village, or York University lots

Alternative Access Points: Finch Station, G Lord Ross Park, Finch West Station

Hiking Options: 4 km: take the subway back from Finch West Station

Biking Options: 13 km (return): turn around at G Lord Ross Park

Connections to Other Routes: 11, 20, 24

On this subway-accessible route, explore York University grounds or Black Creek Pioneer Village before getting on the Black Creek Trail to the Finch Hydro Corridor Trail, also known as the Huron-Wendat Trail for the area's First Nations heritage. Go along the reservoir and dam at G. Lord Ross Park. Have lunch on Yonge Street where there are many options before riding back, hopping on the subway or continuing east for more.

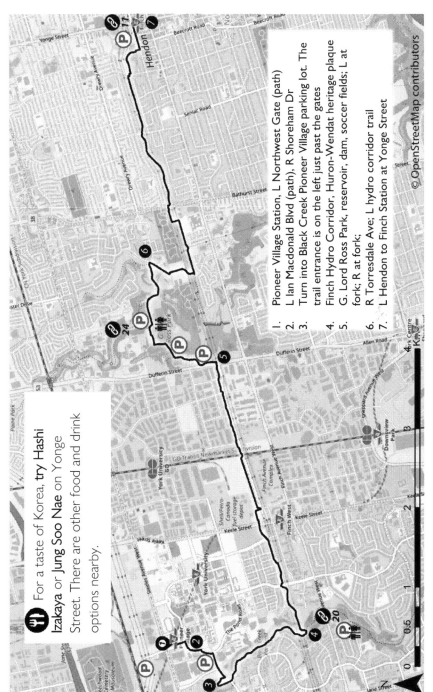

For a taste of Korea, try Hashi Izakaya or Jung Soo Nae on Yonge Street. There are other food and drink options nearby.

1. Pioneer Village Station, L Northwest Gate (path)
2. L Ian Macdonald Blvd (path), R Shoreham Dr
3. Turn into Black Creek Pioneer Village parking lot. The trail entrance is on the left just past the gates
4. Finch Hydro Corridor, Huron-Wendat heritage plaque
5. G. Lord Ross Park, reservoir, dam, soccer fields; L at fork; R at fork;
6. R Torresdale Ave; L hydro corridor trail
7. L Hendon to Finch Station at Yonge Street

© OpenStreetMap contributors

Route 19 – Finch Hydro Corridor West

Scan me

105

Route 20: York U to Downsview Park

Pioneer Village Station to Downsview Park Station

Distance: 11.1 km one-way and return by Subway

Riding Time: 1 hour

Difficulty: Level 1 (Moderate)

Ride Type: Park-Hopper; Cultural Explorer; Foodie

Surface: Paved

Facility Type: 90% path, 10% quiet streets

Elevation Gain/Loss: +/-63 m

Max/Min Grade: 5.6%

Starting Point & Parking: Pay parking at Pioneer Village Station

Alternative Access Points: Pay Parking at Black Creek Pioneer Village, Free parking at Downsview Park

Hiking Options: 6 km return: turn around at Finch; Or start at Downsview Park and explore the hiking trails

Biking Options: Use same path back or a loop via Sentinel Road

Connections to Other Routes: 19

From Black Creek Pioneer Village, follow the Black Creek trail south to Downsview Park, Canada's first urban national park. Do a loop of the park where you'll find a lake, some hiking trails and a children's playground. If you're hungry, check out the international food court and farmer's market, and browse the over 500 vendors at the flea market. End your adventure by either retracing the way you came, making it a loop back with some road connections, or hopping on the subway.

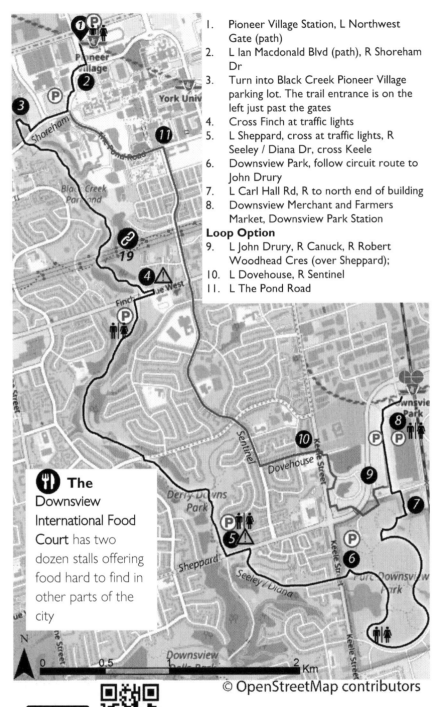

1. Pioneer Village Station, L Northwest Gate (path)
2. L Ian Macdonald Blvd (path), R Shoreham Dr
3. Turn into Black Creek Pioneer Village parking lot. The trail entrance is on the left just past the gates
4. Cross Finch at traffic lights
5. L Sheppard, cross at traffic lights, R Seeley / Diana Dr, cross Keele
6. Downsview Park, follow circuit route to John Drury
7. L Carl Hall Rd, R to north end of building
8. Downsview Merchant and Farmers Market, Downsview Park Station

Loop Option

9. L John Drury, R Canuck, R Robert Woodhead Cres (over Sheppard);
10. L Dovehouse, R Sentinel
11. L The Pond Road

🍴 **The Downsview International Food Court** has two dozen stalls offering food hard to find in other parts of the city

© OpenStreetMap contributors

Route 20 – York U to Downsview

Scan me

CHAPTER

5. NORTH (YORK REGION)

"There is no wifi in the forest, but I promise you will find a better connection."—unknown

York Region spans from the northern edge of Toronto to the southern shores of Lake Simcoe. Much of its area is protected Greenbelt and Oak Ridges Moraine, providing quiet and scenic greenspace and trails. Routes 22, 23, 25, and 26 form part of the Lake to Lake Cycling Route and Walking Trail, an initiative to connect Lake Simcoe to Lake Ontario with a 120 kilometre trail linking communities and destinations along the way.

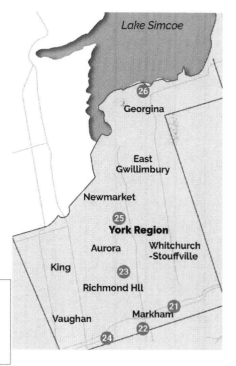

Resources
York Region Cycling Map york.ca/cycling
York Region Trail Guide york.ca/trails
York Region Tourism
experienceyorkregion.com

Route 21: Rouge Valley Trail

Main Street Unionville to Rouge River Community Centre

Distance: 15.8 km return

Riding Time: 1.5 hours

Difficulty: Level 1 (All Ages)

Ride Type: Cultural Explorer, Foodie, Romantic

Surface: Crushed stone

Facility Type: 100% path

Elevation Gain/Loss: +4 m / -10 m (eastbound)

Max/Min Grade: 1.3%

Starting Point & Parking: Main Street Unionville, parking lot on east side behind shops

Alternative Access Points: Rouge River Community Centre, Milne Dam Conservation Park ($)

Hiking Options: Loop around Toogood Pond, north of Unionville Main Street

Biking Options:
- 10 km option – turn around at Milne Dam
- continue south to Bob Hunter Memorial Park and Rouge National Urban Park

Activity: Varley Art Gallery (free admission) at Main St Unionville

Escape to another time at historic Unionville Main Street. Unique shops, ice cream served in every variety and a lively pedestrian atmosphere make Unionville a charming experience. Along the beautiful Rouge Valley Trail, you'll go across bridges, through meadows, under highways, and past a dam. Return back to Unionville with brunch on the patio at Next Door, by the old mill, or an ice cream at Old Firehall Confectionery.

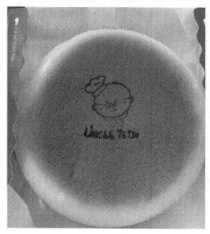

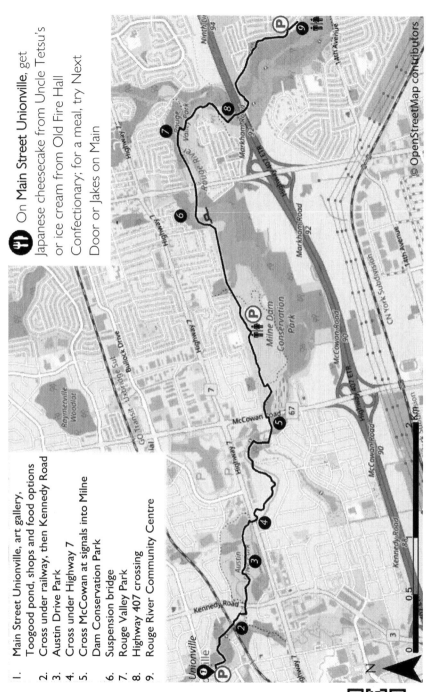

🍴 On Main Street Unionville, get Japanese cheesecake from Uncle Tetsu's or ice cream from Old Fire Hall Confectionary; for a meal, try Next Door or Jakes on Main

1. Main Street Unionville, art gallery, Toogood pond, shops and food options
2. Cross under railway, then Kennedy Road
3. Austin Drive Park
4. Cross under Highway 7
5. Cross McCowan at signals into Milne Dam Conservation Park
6. Suspension bridge
7. Rouge Valley Park
8. Highway 407 crossing
9. Rouge River Community Centre

© OpenStreetMap contributors

Route 21 – Rouge Valley Trail

113

Distance: 10.8 km return;
14.7 km loop option

Riding Time: 1.5 hours

Difficulty: Level 1 (All Ages)

Ride Type: Park-Hopper;
Nature-lover

Surface: Paved

Facility Type: 100% path (out
and back option)

Elevation Gain/Loss:
+9 m / -46 m (southbound)

Max/Min Grade: 4.0%

Starting Point & Parking:
Parking lot at Bayview
Reservoir Park

Alternate Access Points:
On-street parking on Leslie St
at south entrance of German
Mills Settlers Park

Hiking Options: 5 km option,
turn around at Leslie Street

Biking Options: 15 km loop
using East Don Parkland to
Bestview Park and some road
connections

**Connections to Other
Routes:** 10, 11, Lake to Lake
Route

This all ages route will take
you along a hydro corridor
trail through Huntington
Park, a multi-use path on
Leslie Street and John
Street, and a river trail in
German Mills Settlers
Park. There you'll find a
lovely greenspace and
wildlife habitat near
Toronto's border. You can
go back the way you came,
try the loop option if
you're feeling adventurous,
or connect with trails
further south if you're
wanting more.

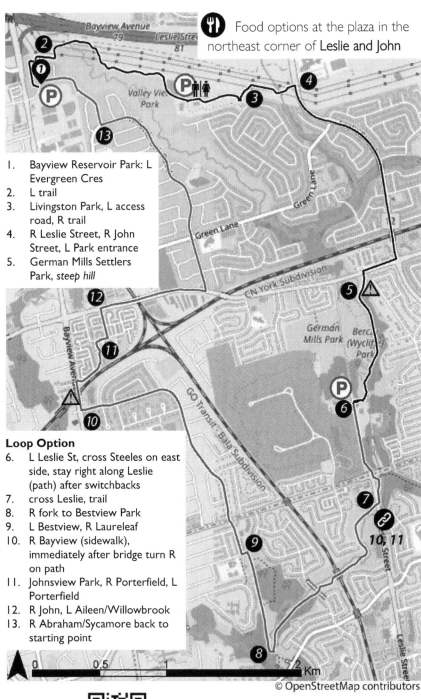

🍴 Food options at the plaza in the northeast corner of **Leslie and John**

1. Bayview Reservoir Park: L Evergreen Cres
2. L trail
3. Livingston Park, L access road, R trail
4. R Leslie Street, R John Street, L Park entrance
5. German Mills Settlers Park, *steep hill*

Loop Option

6. L Leslie St, cross Steeles on east side, stay right along Leslie (path) after switchbacks
7. cross Leslie, trail
8. R fork to Bestview Park
9. L Bestview, R Laureleaf
10. R Bayview (sidewalk), immediately after bridge turn R on path
11. Johnsview Park, R Porterfield, L Porterfield
12. R John, L Aileen/Willowbrook
13. R Abraham/Sycamore back to starting point

© OpenStreetMap contributors

Scan me

Route 22 – Markham Parks

Route 23: Oak Ridges Corridor Loop

Lake Wilcox, to Bathurst St and 19th Avenue

Distance: 20.0 km loop

Riding Time: 2 hours

Difficulty: Level 2 (Moderate)

Ride Type: Nature-lover; Park-Hopper

Surface: Crushed stone

Facility Type: 80% path, 10% quiet streets; 10% bike lanes

Elevation Gain/Loss: +/- 138 m

Max/Min Grade: 4.9%

Starting Point & Parking: Parking lot at Lake Wilcox Park

Alternate Access Points: Parking at Oak Ridges Community Centre; Yonge Street; Bathurst Glen Golf Course; Autumn Grove Park

Hiking Options: 6 km loop by taking the fork right after Bayview bridge to Old Colony Road

Biking Options: 12 km (return): turn around at Bond Lake / Yonge Street

Connections to Other Routes: Lake to Lake Route

This tour starts at beautiful Lake Wilcox Park in Richmond Hill. Travel through the Oak Ridges Corridor Conservation Reserve, a rich natural area that includes wetlands, kettle lakes and forests. The trail will take you past Bond Lake, which has First Nations heritage dating back thousands of years. Connect to the Saigeon Trail that features a pond and river. End the loop with a picnic and cool off in the splash pad.

Activities:
Richmond Hill Canoe Club rents canoes and kayaks on weekends in the summer from 1-6 pm (rhcc.on.ca); geocaching (geocaching.com)

117

🍴 Stop for a snack at **Bathurst Glen Golf Course** clubhouse; if doing the loop option, consider a detour to Tower Hill Road for Starbucks, Turtle Jack's or Sunset Grill at Yonge Street.

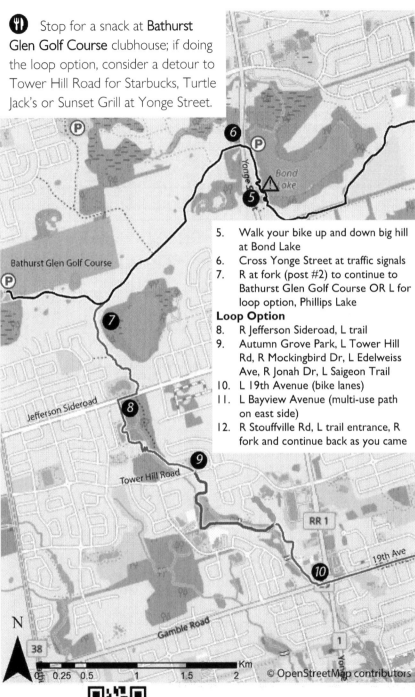

5. Walk your bike up and down big hill at Bond Lake
6. Cross Yonge Street at traffic signals
7. R at fork (post #2) to continue to Bathurst Glen Golf Course OR L for loop option, Phillips Lake

Loop Option

8. R Jefferson Sideroad, L trail
9. Autumn Grove Park, L Tower Hill Rd, R Mockingbird Dr, L Edelweiss Ave, R Jonah Dr, L Saigeon Trail
10. L 19th Avenue (bike lanes)
11. L Bayview Avenue (multi-use path on east side)
12. R Stouffville Rd, L trail entrance, R fork and continue back as you came

© OpenStreetMap contributors

Route 23 – Oak Ridges Corridor (1 of 2)

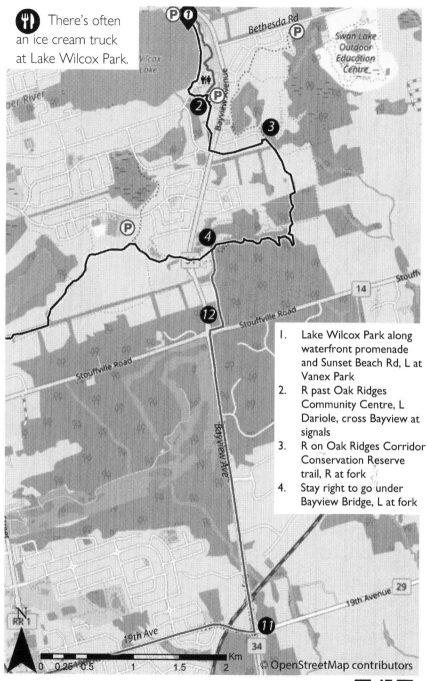

There's often an ice cream truck at Lake Wilcox Park.

1. Lake Wilcox Park along waterfront promenade and Sunset Beach Rd, L at Vanex Park
2. R past Oak Ridges Community Centre, L Dariole, cross Bayview at signals
3. R on Oak Ridges Corridor Conservation Reserve trail, R at fork
4. Stay right to go under Bayview Bridge, L at fork

© OpenStreetMap contributors

Route 23 – Oak Ridges Corridor (1 of 2)

121

Route 24: Bartley Smith Greenway

Rutherford GO Station to
G. Lord Ross Park

Distance: 24.8 km return

Riding Time: 2.5 hours

Difficulty: Level 2 (Moderate)

Ride Type: Park-Hopper;
Nature-lover

Surface: Paved south of
Steeles; crushed stone north of
Steeles, concrete through
Marita Payne Park

Facility Type: 90% path, 10%
quiet strets

Elevation Gain/Loss: +7 m /
-36 m (southbound)

Max/Min Grade: 2.9%

Starting Point & Parking:
Rutherford GO Station

Alternate Access Points:
Parking at G. Lord Ross Park;
Dufferin Clark Community
Centre

Hiking Options: 5 km return:
turn around at Planchet Rd; 10
km return: turn around at
Rivermede Road/Keffer Marsh

Biking Options: 18 km
return: turn around at Steeles

**Connections to Other
Routes:** 19

Follow the Lower Bartley
Smith Greenway along the
West Don River. You'll
pass Langstaff EcoPark, a
natural regeneration area,
and Keffer Marsh where
you can look for beavers,
mink, snakes, turtles, frogs
and many species of birds.
Picnic at G. Lord Ross
Park before heading back,
or for a change of scenery,
continue west along the
Finch Hydro Corridor
Trail and take the Keele
bus or GO Train back
from York University.

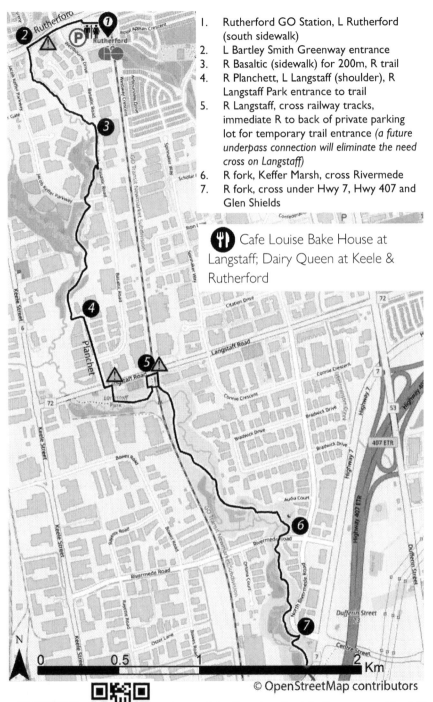

1. Rutherford GO Station, L Rutherford (south sidewalk)
2. L Bartley Smith Greenway entrance
3. R Basaltic (sidewalk) for 200m, R trail
4. R Planchett, L Langstaff (shoulder), R Langstaff Park entrance to trail
5. R Langstaff, cross railway tracks, immediate R to back of private parking lot for temporary trail entrance (*a future underpass connection will eliminate the need cross on Langstaff*)
6. R fork, Keffer Marsh, cross Rivermede
7. R fork, cross under Hwy 7, Hwy 407 and Glen Shields

🍴 Cafe Louise Bake House at Langstaff; Dairy Queen at Keele & Rutherford

© OpenStreetMap contributors

Route 24 – Bartley Smith Greenway (1 of 2)

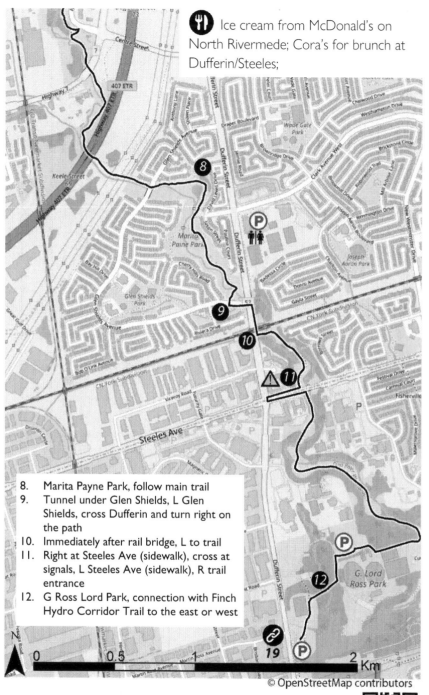

🍴 Ice cream from McDonald's on North Rivermede; Cora's for brunch at Dufferin/Steeles;

8. Marita Payne Park, follow main trail
9. Tunnel under Glen Shields, L Glen Shields, cross Dufferin and turn right on the path
10. Immediately after rail bridge, L to trail
11. Right at Steeles Ave (sidewalk), cross at signals, L Steeles Ave (sidewalk), R trail entrance
12. G Ross Lord Park, connection with Finch Hydro Corridor Trail to the east or west

© OpenStreetMap contributors

Route 24 – Bartley Smith Greenway (2 of 2)

Route 25:
Nokiidaa Trail

Aurora GO Station to
Holland Landing

Essentials

Distance: 37 km return

Riding Time: 3.5 hours

Difficulty: Level 3 (Fit)

Ride Type: Park-Hopper, Cultural Explorer, Foodie

Surface: Aurora is crushed stone; Newmarket is paved; East Gwillimbury is dirt, boardwalk, and crushed stone

Facility Type: 98% path, 2% road connections

Elevation Gain/Loss: +56 m / -103 m (northbound)

Max/Min Grade: 9.4%

Starting Point & Parking: Aurora GO Station Parking Lot

Alternate Access Points: Newmarket Riverwalk Commons, Newmarket GO Station, East Gwillimbury GO Station, Yonge & Mount Albert

Hiking Options: Sheppard's Bush Conservation Area, Roger's Reservoir CA

Biking Options: 15 km (return): Riverwalk Commons north to Yonge and Mount Albert

Connections to Other Routes: Lake to Lake Route

The Nokiidaa Trail links the Towns of Aurora, Newmarket and East Gwillimbury following the East Holland River. The trail passes through town parks, natural spaces, and historic cultural sites. It's great for all ages since there are few road crossings. There are many access points, so pick a segment or do the whole thing. Stop at historic Main Street Newmarket to explore the shops, heritage museum and restaurants and have a famous butter tart at Maid's Cottage. Go through the popular Roger's Reservoir Conservation Area and see remains of the partially constructed "ghost canal" at the 2nd Concession bridge. Have lunch at Chefies Eatery in Holland Landing before heading back.

The **2nd Concession** bridge and boardwalk in Roger's Reservoir Conservation Area

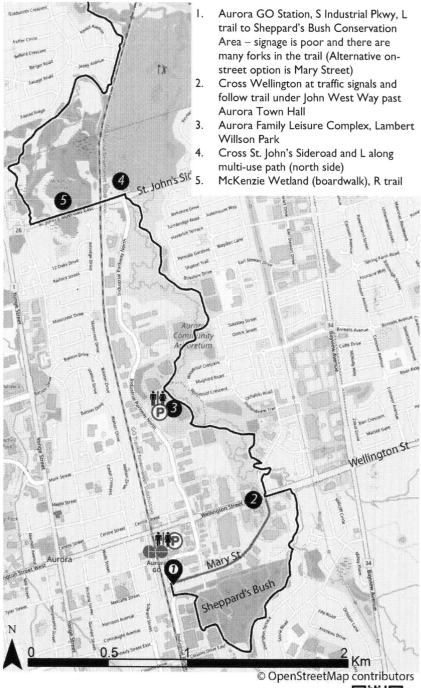

1. Aurora GO Station, S Industrial Pkwy, L trail to Sheppard's Bush Conservation Area – signage is poor and there are many forks in the trail (Alternative on-street option is Mary Street)
2. Cross Wellington at traffic signals and follow trail under John West Way past Aurora Town Hall
3. Aurora Family Leisure Complex, Lambert Willson Park
4. Cross St. John's Sideroad and L along multi-use path (north side)
5. McKenzie Wetland (boardwalk), R trail

© OpenStreetMap contributors

Route 25 – Nokiidaa Trail (1 of 3)

Scan me

129

🍽 Main Street Newmarket has many wonderful lunch options like the patio at Cachet Restaurant at Fairy Lake; **Saturday farmer's market at Riverwalk Commons** in Newmarket

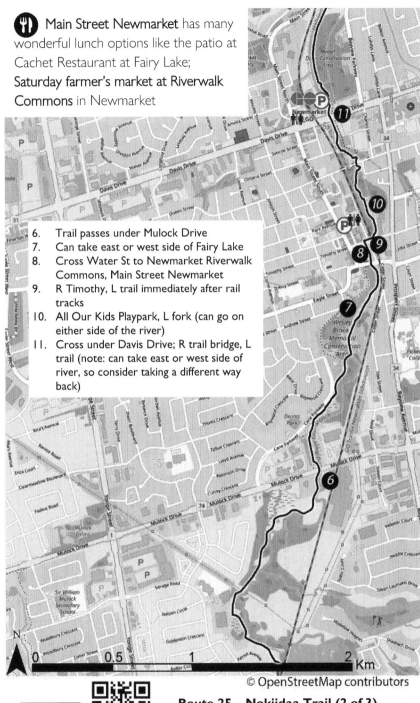

6. Trail passes under Mulock Drive
7. Can take east or west side of Fairy Lake
8. Cross Water St to Newmarket Riverwalk Commons, Main Street Newmarket
9. R Timothy, L trail immediately after rail tracks
10. All Our Kids Playpark, L fork (can go on either side of the river)
11. Cross under Davis Drive; R trail bridge, L trail (note: can take east or west side of river, so consider taking a different way back)

© OpenStreetMap contributors

Route 25 – Nokiidaa Trail (2 of 3)

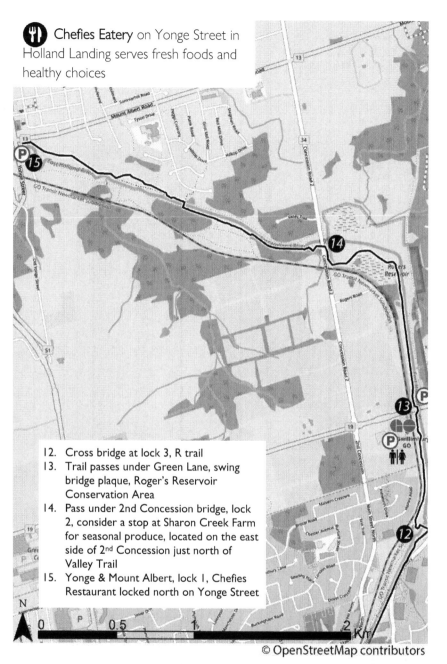

🍴 **Chefies Eatery** on Yonge Street in Holland Landing serves fresh foods and healthy choices

12. Cross bridge at lock 3, R trail
13. Trail passes under Green Lane, swing bridge plaque, Roger's Reservoir Conservation Area
14. Pass under 2nd Concession bridge, lock 2, consider a stop at Sharon Creek Farm for seasonal produce, located on the east side of 2ⁿᵈ Concession just north of Valley Trail
15. Yonge & Mount Albert, lock 1, Chefies Restaurant locked north on Yonge Street

© OpenStreetMap contributors

Route 25 – Nokiidaa Trail (3 of 3)

Route 26: Lake Simcoe Beaches
The ROC to Sibbald Point Provincial Park

Essentials

Distance: 28.2 km return

Riding Time: 2.5 hours

Difficulty: Level 2 (Moderate)

Ride Type: Park-Hopper; Romantic, Cultural Explorer

Surface: Paved

Facility Type: 5% path, 95% quiet streets

Elevation Gain/Loss: +78 m / - 80 m (eastbound)

Max/Min Grade: 3.4%

Starting Point & Parking: Recreation Outdoor Campus (The ROC)

Alternate Access Points: Willow Beach Park ($), Willow Wharf Park ($), De La Salle Park ($), Sibbald Point Provincial Park ($)

Hiking Options: Trails at the ROC and Sibbald Point Provincial Park

Biking Options: 17 km (return): turn around at Jackson's Point

Connections to Other Routes: Lake to Lake Route

Start your tour at The Recreation Outdoor Campus (ROC) which includes a splash pad, bike pump track and pioneer village. Follow the Lake Simcoe shoreline and stop at several beaches along the way. The wharf is a perfect spot to enjoy an ice cream treat from the snack shop, or refuel at the restaurants at Jackson's Point. At Sibbald Point Provincial Park, explore the trails, cool off in the water, or relax on the beach. This is a fun family adventure.

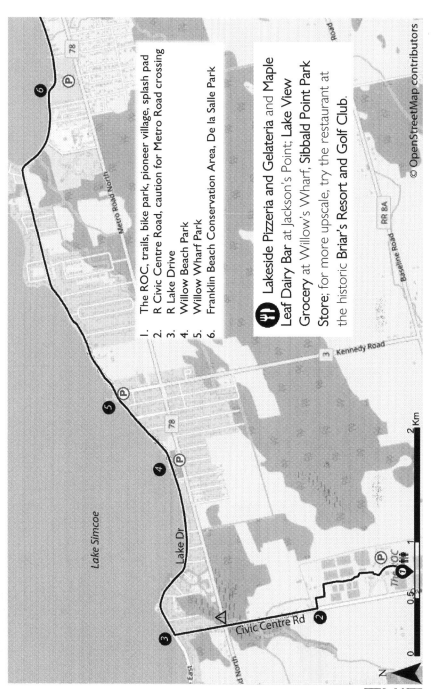

1. The ROC, trails, bike park, pioneer village, splash pad
2. R Civic Centre Road, caution for Metro Road crossing
3. R Lake Drive
4. Willow Beach Park
5. Willow Wharf Park
6. Franklin Beach Conservation Area, De la Salle Park

🍴 Lakeside Pizzeria and Gelateria and Maple Leaf Dairy Bar at Jackson's Point; Lake View Grocery at Willow's Wharf, Sibbald Point Park Store; for more upscale, try the restaurant at the historic Briar's Resort and Golf Club.

© OpenStreetMap contributors

Route 26 – Lake Simcoe Beaches (1 of 2)

Scan me

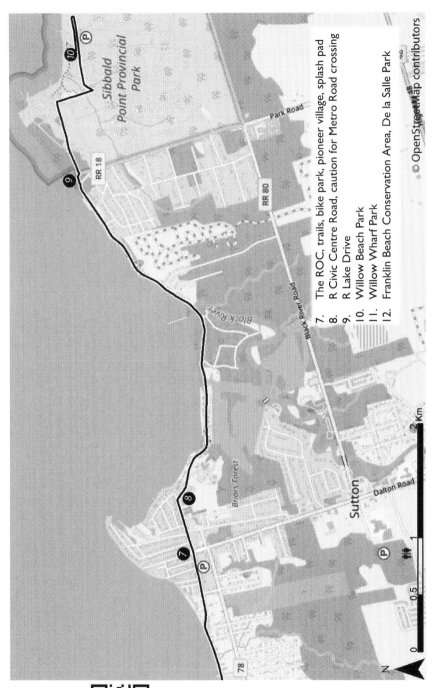

© OpenStreetMap contributors

7. The ROC, trails, bike park, pioneer village, splash pad
8. R Civic Centre Road, caution for Metro Road crossing
9. R Lake Drive
10. Willow Beach Park
11. Willow Wharf Park
12. Franklin Beach Conservation Area, De la Salle Park

Route 26 – Lake Simcoe Beaches (2 of 2)

CHAPTER

6. EAST (DURHAM REGION)

"If a child is to keep alive his inborn sense of wonder, they need the companionship of at least one adult who can share it, rediscovering with them the joy, excitement and mystery of the world we live in."—Rachel Carson

Durham Region's north is mostly rural and contains the rolling hills of the Oak Ridges Moraine, while the south has thriving urban communities and the

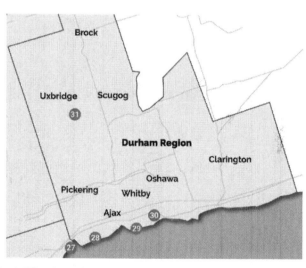

Waterfront Trail. The first three routes in this chapter feature the Waterfront Trail, a wonderful place to bike and hike!

Resources
Durham Region Trails durham.ca/en/tourism/trails-and-conservation-areas.aspx
Durham Region Trail Map maps.durham.ca/TrailsMap/default.html

Route 27: Rouge to Pickering Waterfront

Rouge GO Station to Rotary Park in Ajax

Distance: 29.8 km return

Riding Time: 3 hours

Difficulty: Level 2 (Moderate)

Ride Type: Park-Hopper, Cultural Explorer

Surface: Paved

Facility Type:

Elevation Gain/Loss: +34 m / -37 m (eastbound)

Max/Min Grade: 3.4%

Starting Point & Parking: Rouge Hill GO Station

Alternate Access Points: Pickering GO Station, Petticoat Creek Conservation Area, Rotary Park

Hiking Options: 7 km (return): to Petticoat Creek Conservation Area

Biking Options: 8 km to Pickering GO Station; 12 km (return): to the end of the pier at Frenchman's Bay; 20 km (return) to Millenium Square

Connections to Other Routes: 13, 28

Start at the Rouge Hill GO Station just steps from the Waterfront Trail and head east, where you'll get unobstructed views of the lake. Consider going to the end of the pier at Frenchman's Bay before going around the bay. Picnic at Petticoat Creek Conservation Area or award-winning Millenium Square beachfront, or dine on The Waterfront restaurant rooftop patio overlooking the marina. Take the train back from Pickering GO or continue on to Ajax. This is a fun ride!

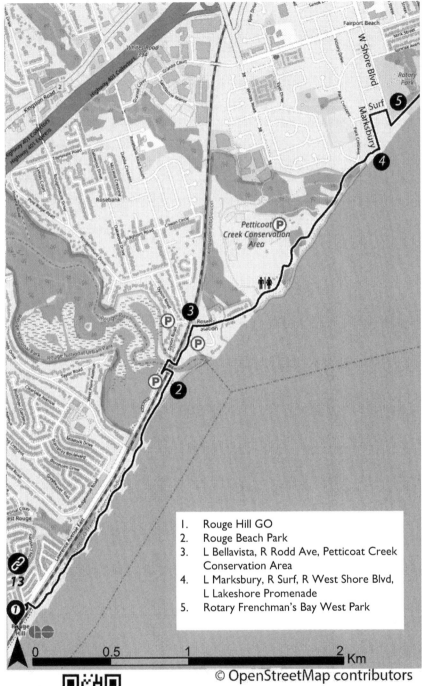

1. Rouge Hill GO
2. Rouge Beach Park
3. L Bellavista, R Rodd Ave, Petticoat Creek Conservation Area
4. L Marksbury, R Surf, R West Shore Blvd, L Lakeshore Promenade
5. Rotary Frenchman's Bay West Park

© OpenStreetMap contributors

 Scan me

Route 27 –
Rouge to Pickering Waterfront (1 of 2)

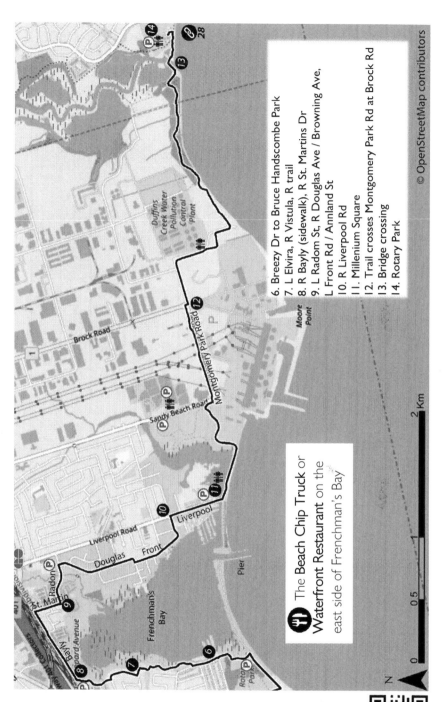

6. Breezy Dr to Bruce Handscombe Park
7. L Elvira, R Vistula, R trail
8. R Bayly (sidewalk), R St. Martins Dr
9. L Radom St, R Douglas Ave / Browning Ave, L Front Rd / Annland St
10. R Liverpool Rd
11. Millenium Square
12. Trail crosses Montgomery Park Rd at Brock Rd
13. Bridge crossing
14. Rotary Park

🍴 The Beach Chip Truck or Waterfront Restaurant on the east side of Frenchman's Bay

© OpenStreetMap contributors

Route 27 –
Rouge to Pickering Waterfront (2 of 2)

Route 28: Ajax Loop

Duffins Creek to Clement St to Greenbelt Trail to Waterfront Trail

Distance: 10.4 km loop

Riding Time: 1 hour

Difficulty: Level 2 (Moderate)

Ride Type: Park-Hopper, Romantic

Surface: Paved along waterfront, dirt along Duffins Creek

Facility Type: 76% path, 24% bike lanes and quiet streets

Elevation Gain/Loss: +/- 22m

Max/Min Grade: 6.7%

Starting Point & Parking: Rotary Park

Alternate Access Points: Ajax Community Centre, Veterans Point Gardens, Ajax GO Station

Hiking Options: 4 km return: Duffins Creek Trail

Biking Options: 7 km return: Waterfront Trail to Paradise Park

Connections to Other Routes: 27, 29

This loop offers a great opportunity to explore Ajax. Start at Rotary Park with easy access to the creek at the edge of Lake Ontario. Bike or hike along Duffins Creek, part of the Trans Canada Trail. The waterfront trail through Ajax is all off-road public parkland. At the foot of Harwood Ave is Veterans Point Gardens, dedicated to HMS Ajax, the Royal Navy ship after which the Town was named. End the loop back at Rotary Park, with a splash pad, playground, view of the lake and great place for a picnic.

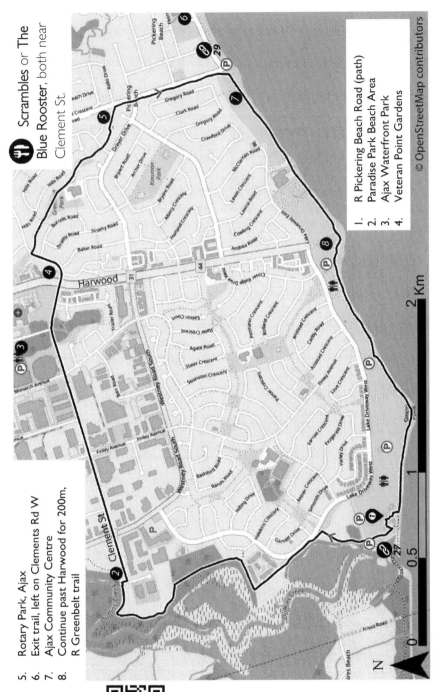

Scrambles or The Blue Rooster, both near Clement St.

1. R Pickering Beach Road (path)
2. Paradise Park Beach Area
3. Ajax Waterfront Park
4. Veteran Point Gardens

5. Rotary Park, Ajax
6. Exit trail, left on Clements Rd W
7. Ajax Community Centre
8. Continue past Harwood for 200m, R Greenbelt trail

© OpenStreetMap contributors

Scan me

Route 28 – Ajax Loop

Route 29: Ajax to Oshawa Waterfront

Rotary Park to Lakeview Park

Distance: 51.8 km return

Riding Time: 5 hours

Difficulty: Level 3 (Fit)

Ride Type: Park-Hopper, Foodie, Romantic

Surface: Paved

Facility Type: 62% path, 38% quiet streets

Elevation Gain/Loss: +26 m / - 26 m (eastbound)

Max/Min Grade: 2.0%

Starting Point & Parking: Rotary Park in Ajax

Alternate Access Points:

Hiking Options: Nature trails and lookouts connected to the waterfront through Lynde Shores Conservation Area.

Biking Options:

Connections to Other Routes: 27, 28, 30

Activities: The Rowe House, the first mayor's house, is open for you to explore Whitby's history; Beaches at Lake Park and Heydenshore Kiwanis Park; birding in Thickson's Woods; Oshawa Museum

Park-hop to your heart's content on this popular trail. This tour has some of the best waterfront trail along Lake Ontario. If you make it all the way to Lakeview Park in Oshawa, have an ice cream or lunch at Tommy's Homemade Fries before heading back. Enjoy the beautiful natural areas like Lynde Shore Conservation Area and Thickson's Woods, the last remnant of old-growth white pines on the north shore of Lake Ontario. Consider camping to the east at Darlington Provincial Park.

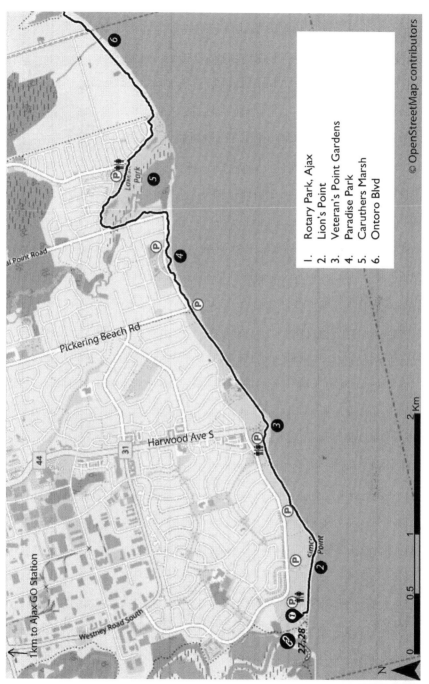

© OpenStreetMap contributors

1. Rotary Park, Ajax
2. Lion's Point
3. Veteran's Point Gardens
4. Paradise Park
5. Caruthers Marsh
6. Ontoro Blvd

**Route 29 –
Ajax to Oshawa Waterfront (1 of 3)**

147

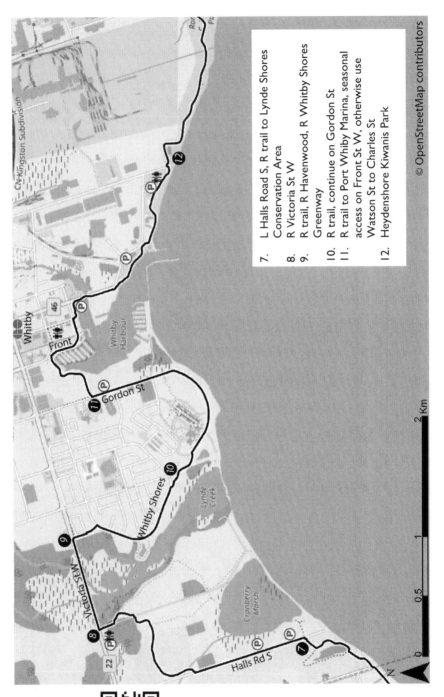

7. L Halls Road S, R trail to Lynde Shores Conservation Area
8. R Victoria St W
9. R trail, R Havenwood, R Whitby Shores Greenway
10. R trail, continue on Gordon St
11. R trail to Port Whiby Marina, seasonal access on Front St W, otherwise use Watson St to Charles St
12. Heydenshore Kiwanis Park

© OpenStreetMap contributors

Scan me

148

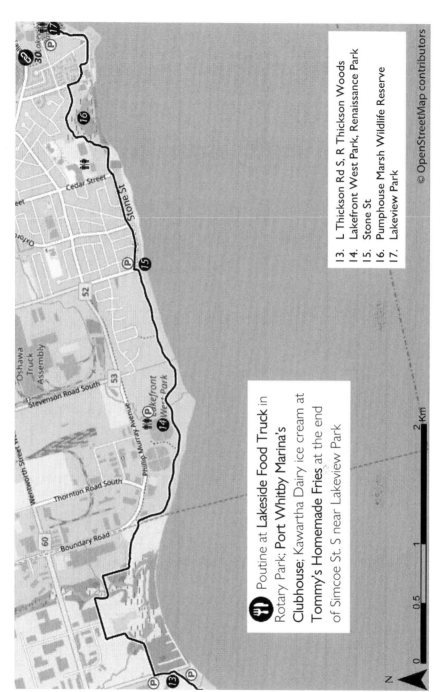

13. L Thickson Rd S, R Thickson Woods
14. Lakefront West Park, Renaissance Park
15. Stone St
16. Pumphouse Marsh Wildlife Reserve
17. Lakeview Park

Poutine at Lakeside Food Truck in Rotary Park; Port Whitby Marina's Clubhouse; Kawartha Dairy ice cream at Tommy's Homemade Fries at the end of Simcoe St. S near Lakeview Park

© OpenStreetMap contributors

Route 29 –
Ajax to Oshawa Waterfront (3 of 3)

Route 30: Oshawa Creek

Oshawa Civic Centre to
Lake Ontario Waterfront

Distance: 11.0 km return

Riding Time: 1 hour

Difficulty: Level 1 (All Ages)

Ride Type: Park-hopper;
Cultural Explorer

Surface: Paved

Facility Type: 100% path

Elevation Gain/Loss:
0 m / - 31 m (southbound)

Max/Min Grade: 3.8%

Starting Point & Parking:
Oshawa Civic Centre

Alternate Access Points:
Lakeview Park

Hiking Options: 2km: north
to Oshawa Valley Botanical
Gardens

Biking Options: 8km return:
start at Storie Park

**Connections to Other
Routes:** 29

Activities: Oshawa Valley
Botanical Garden is worth a
visit and found a further 800m
north of the Civic Centre, on
the trail; Robert McLaughlin
Gallery near the Civic Centre;

This is a trail for the whole family that's worth putting your bikes on the car and travelling to. Ride the Joseph Kolodzie Trail from downtown Oshawa as it gently declines along Oshawa Creek to Lake Ontario. You'll use many bridges and tunnels and eventually be greeted by a fine view of the lake. Visit some historical homes at the Oshawa museum or go for a swim in the lake before heading back. Or, if you want to extend the ride, go east or west along the Waterfront Trail.

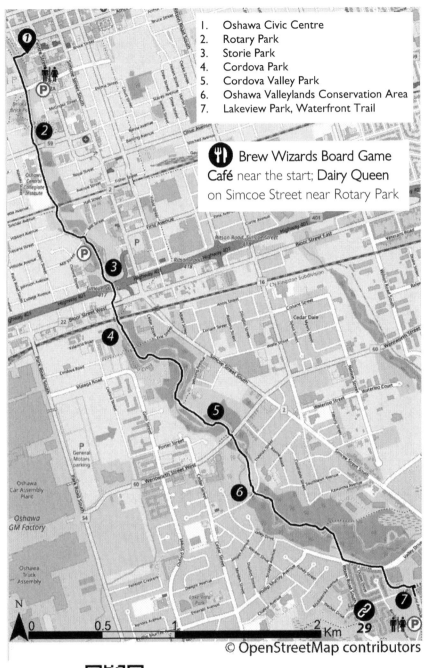

1. Oshawa Civic Centre
2. Rotary Park
3. Storie Park
4. Cordova Park
5. Cordova Valley Park
6. Oshawa Valleylands Conservation Area
7. Lakeview Park, Waterfront Trail

🍴 **Brew Wizards Board Game Café** near the start; **Dairy Queen** on Simcoe Street near Rotary Park

© OpenStreetMap contributors

Route 30 – Oshawa Creek

Route 31: Uxbridge to Lindsay
Rail Trail

Distance: 44.8 km one way, 89.6 km return

Riding Time: 8 hours

Difficulty: Level 3 (Fit)

Ride Type: Nature-lover; Cultural explorer

Surface: Crushed stone

Facility Type: 99% path, 1% quiet roads

Elevation Gain/Loss: +123 m / -127 m (northbound)

Max/Min Grade: 1.5%

Starting Point & Parking: York-Durham Heritage Railway, municipal parking lot at Toronto St N & Albert

Alternate Access Points: Could also park in Uxbridge on the side streets by 2nd Ave and Rosena Lane

Hiking Options: Out and back however long you feel like

Biking Options: 39 km return: Uxbridge to Sunderland; consider a car shuttle for a one-way tour

Connections to Other Routes: Trans Canada Trail (The Great Trail)

This bikes, trains, and automobiles tour is good for a family outing or a long cross-country trek for the adventurous types, as Lindsay is a long way! Start at the York-Durham Heritage Railway station where you can visit the on-site museum and see a vintage train. You'll pass over a historic trestle bridge near the start of the trail. It's fairly flat and there are lots of forests, marshes and farm fields to gaze upon. Go as far as you like and enjoy the solitude of nature. Make it a multi-day trip with an overnight stay in Lindsay at the Days Inn and Suites, located by the trail. For a shorter option, take the fork left to Sunderland for lunch and make it a 39 km roundtrip from Uxbridge.

153

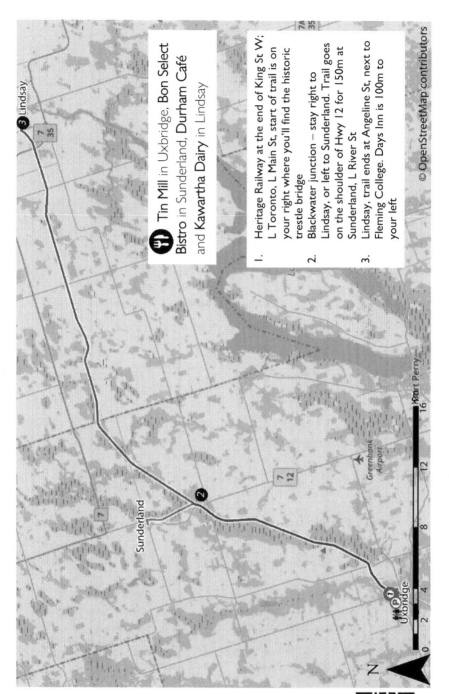

🍴 Tin Mill in Uxbridge, Bon Select Bistro in Sunderland, Durham Café and Kawartha Dairy in Lindsay

1. Heritage Railway at the end of King St W; L Toronto, L Main St, start of trail is on your right where you'll find the historic trestle bridge

2. Blackwater junction – stay right to Lindsay, or left to Sunderland. Trail goes on the shoulder of Hwy 12 for 150m at Sunderland, L River St

3. Lindsay, trail ends at Angeline St, next to Fleming College. Days Inn is 100m to your left

© OpenStreetMap contributors

Route 31 – Uxbridge to Lindsay

155

"You're off to Great Places!
Today is your day!
Your mountain is waiting,
So…get on your way!"
—Dr. Seuss, Oh, The Places You'll Go!

CHAPTER

7. WEST (PEEL REGION, HALTON REGION, CITY OF HAMILTON)

"We do not take a trip… a trip takes us."—John Steinbeck

This chapter includes routes in Peel Region, Halton Region and the City of Hamilton. Whether you choose the Lake Ontario Waterfront Trail (Routes 32, 38, 39), a river trail (Routes 33, 34, 37), or a rail trail (Routes 35, 36, 40), you're sure to have a memorable adventure.

Resources
Peel Region Trails walkandrollpeel.ca
Halton conservationhalton.ca/hiking
Hamilton-Burlington Trails hamiltonburlingtontrails.ca
Hamilton Bike Share hamilton.socialbicycles.com

Route 32: Mississauga Waterfront

Marie Curtis Park to Jack Darling Park

Distance: 23.6 km return

Riding Time: 2.5 hours

Difficulty: Level 2 (Moderate)

Ride Type: Park-Hopper; Foodie; Romantic

Surface: Paved

Facility Type: 70% path, 27% quiet streets, 3% busy roads (bike lane)

Elevation Gain/Loss: +/-15m

Max/Min Grade: 2.6%

Starting Point & Parking: Marie Curtis Park or Long Branch GO Station

Alternate Access Points: Jack Darling Park, Lakefront Promenade Park

Hiking Options: 5 km (return): St. Lawrence park west to Rhododendron Gardens; Consider a hike through Rattray Marsh from Jack Darling Park

Biking Options: 16 km (return): turn around a Port Credit

Connections to Other Routes: 14

A trip along this beautifully designed stretch of waterfront is a memorable one. Have a break at one of the many cafes and restaurants in historic Port Credit Village, and see one of the last remaining coastal wetlands along Lake Ontario at Rattray Marsh. Along the way, wander the many parks, tour the historical architecture at the Adamson Estate, dip in a splash pad and delight in the many opportunities to hear the waves of Lake Ontario lapping the shore.

158

Snug Harbour, right off the trail, has a patio and lake view and serves excellent family fare at moderate prices. Many other food options **on Lakeshore Road in Port Credit**.

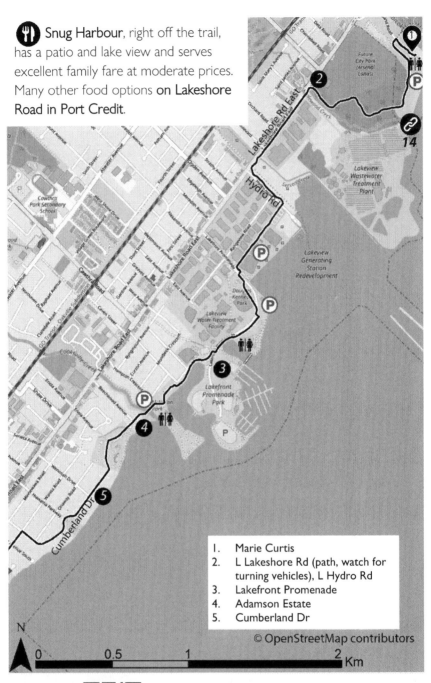

1. Marie Curtis
2. L Lakeshore Rd (path, watch for turning vehicles), L Hydro Rd
3. Lakefront Promenade
4. Adamson Estate
5. Cumberland Dr

© OpenStreetMap contributors

Route 32 – Mississauga Waterfront (1 of 2)

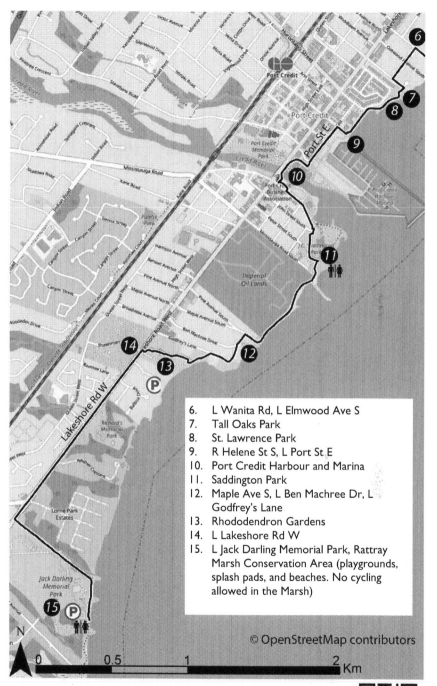

6. L Wanita Rd, L Elmwood Ave S
7. Tall Oaks Park
8. St. Lawrence Park
9. R Helene St S, L Port St E
10. Port Credit Harbour and Marina
11. Saddington Park
12. Maple Ave S, L Ben Machree Dr, L Godfrey's Lane
13. Rhododendron Gardens
14. L Lakeshore Rd W
15. L Jack Darling Memorial Park, Rattray Marsh Conservation Area (playgrounds, splash pads, and beaches. No cycling allowed in the Marsh)

© OpenStreetMap contributors

0   0.5   1   2 Km

Route 32 – Mississauga Waterfront (2 of 2)

Route 33: Etobicoke Creek

Downtown Brampton to Centennial Park in Toronto

Distance: 41.8 km return

Riding Time: 4 hours

Difficulty: Level 3 (Fit)

Ride Type: Park-Hopper; Cultural Explorer

Surface: Mix of paved and crushed stone

Facility Type: 84% path, 13% quiet streets, 3% busy roads

Elevation Gain/Loss: +11m / -87 m (southbound)

Max/Min Grade: 4.2%

Starting Point & Parking: Gage Park. Parking is available across the street underneath City Hall, free on weekends.

Alternate Access Points: Centennial Park (off of Mary St) in Brampton, Brampton GO Station, Centennial Park in Toronto, Renforth MiWay

Hiking Options: 4 km loop to Charles Watson and using Main Street on the return

Biking Options: 9 km return: turn around at Steeles; 46 km to Union Station, take train back to Brampton GO Station

Connections to Other Routes: 18, 34

This adventure starts at popular Gage Park in downtown Brampton, continues into Mississauga on the first public trail in Canada to pass through airport land, and ends up at Centennial Park at the edge of Toronto. Visit the conservatory which has three areas: a greenhouse with 200 varieties of tropical plants, an arid house which has cacti and succulents, and a display house with local shrubs and plants. Upon your return to Brampton, there are many cafes, restaurants, or ice cream options in the area.

1. Gage Park, east on Wellington St
2. R Mary St, L Centennial Park
3. Charles F Watson Family Gardens
4. loop under Steeles bridge, R Steeles (sidewalk)
5. R path connection, L Austin Dr, R path
6. Kennedy Road, cross at signals
7. Continue under Hwy 410, 407, Mount Charles Park

Brampton's downtown farmer's market held every Saturday morning in Garden Square, and many nearby food options like Poutine Dare to be Fresh, Freshly Thai and Ice Cream Cafe

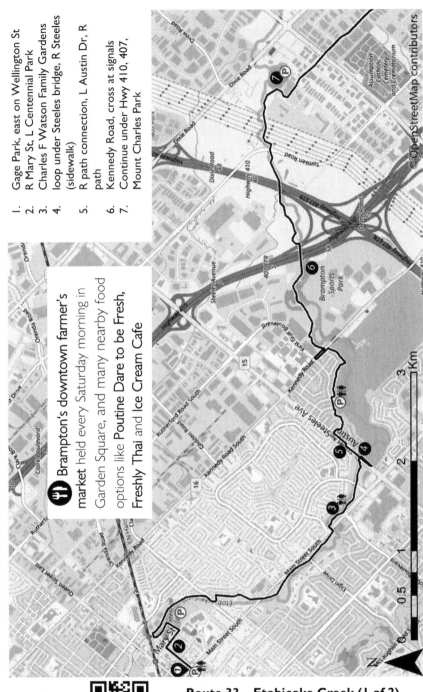

© OpenStreetMap contributors

Scan me

Route 33 – Etobicoke Creek (1 of 2)

While in the airport land, which is opened from dawn to dusk, very specific rules apply and will be strictly enforced by Airport Security, so while on the trail do not:

- litter, dump trash of other waste
- picnic or feed animals
- use any drones
- camp or park overnight

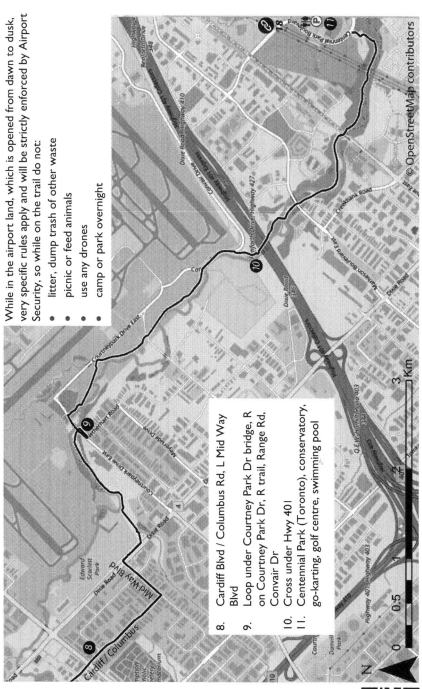

8. Cardiff Blvd / Columbus Rd, L Mid Way Blvd
9. Loop under Courtney Park Dr bridge, R on Courtney Park Dr, R trail, Range Rd, Convair Dr
10. Cross under Hwy 401
11. Centennial Park (Toronto), conservatory, go-karting, golf centre, swimming pool

© OpenStreetMap contributors

Route 33 – Etobicoke Creek (2 of 2)

Route 34: Upper Etobicoke Creek

Loafer's Lake to Downtown Brampton

Essentials

Distance: 13.6 km return

Riding Time: 1.5 hours

Difficulty: Level 1 (All Ages)

Ride Type: Park-Hopper, Cultural Explorer

Surface: Paved

Facility Type: 97% path, 3% quiet streets

Elevation Gain/Loss: +5m /-28m (southbound)

Max/Min Grade: 2.0%

Starting Point & Parking: Loafer's Lake Recreation Centre

Alternate Access Points: Rosalea Park Parking Lot (Church St, east of Main St N), Brampton GO Station

Hiking Options: Loop around Loafer's Lake

Biking Options: Trail continues north of Loafer's Lake or south of downtown; 40km option – Bike the Creek route (annual event in June) links Etobicoke Creek Trail with Chinguacousy Trail

Connections to Other Routes: 33

Follow the greenway path as it meanders the Etobicoke Creek. There are very few road crossings as the trail passes under several bridges and eventually takes you to Garden Square in downtown Brampton. There you can visit a variety of cultural activities like the Peel Region museum, art gallery, and farmer's market held every Saturday morning, or have a close-up look at some historical buildings. Treat yourself to poutine, ice cream, macaroons and more before making the return trip.

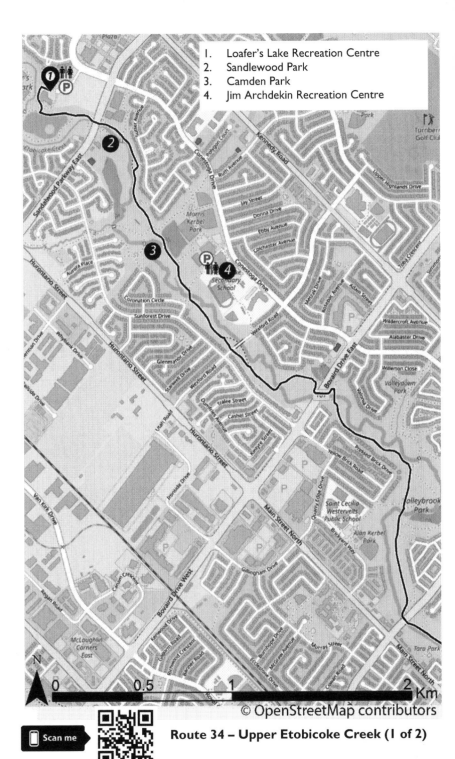

1. Loafer's Lake Recreation Centre
2. Sandlewood Park
3. Camden Park
4. Jim Archdekin Recreation Centre

© OpenStreetMap contributors

Route 34 – Upper Etobicoke Creek (1 of 2)

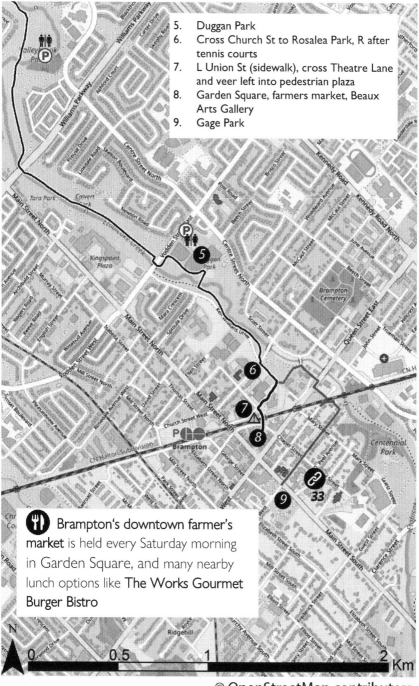

5. Duggan Park
6. Cross Church St to Rosalea Park, R after tennis courts
7. L Union St (sidewalk), cross Theatre Lane and veer left into pedestrian plaza
8. Garden Square, farmers market, Beaux Arts Gallery
9. Gage Park

🍴 **Brampton's downtown farmer's market** is held every Saturday morning in Garden Square, and many nearby lunch options like **The Works Gourmet Burger Bistro**

© OpenStreetMap contributors

Route 34 – Upper Etobicoke Creek (2 of 2)

Scan me

Route 35: Tottenham to Caledon
Caledon Trailway

Here's a perfect trail adventure for families or new riders. The Caledon Trailway follows an abandoned railway line. Start at the northeast end of the trail in Tottenham, where you can take a one hour ride on a restored vintage locomotive. Head southwest on the trail through Palgrave to Canada's first Great Trail Pavilion at Caledon East. Have lunch at Tom's Family Restaurant or a treat at Four Corners Bakery before heading back through farm fields, woodlots, and across the deep Humber River Valley. Those wanting a longer tour can continue west all the way to Terra Cotta, stopping at Spirit Tree Estate Cidery and Cheltenham badlands.

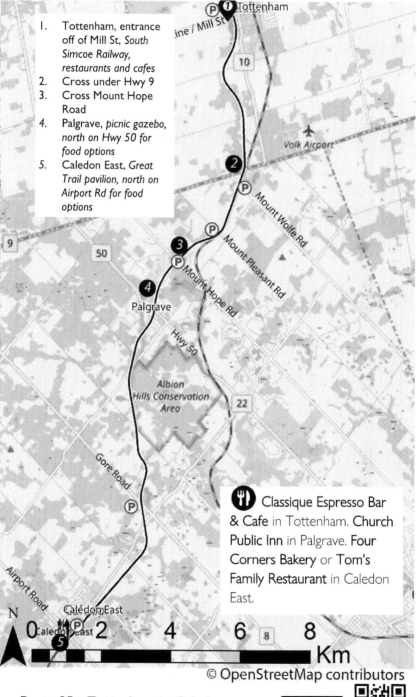

1. Tottenham, entrance off of Mill St, *South Simcoe Railway, restaurants and cafes*
2. Cross under Hwy 9
3. Cross Mount Hope Road
4. Palgrave, *picnic gazebo, north on Hwy 50 for food options*
5. Caledon East, *Great Trail pavilion, north on Airport Rd for food options*

Classique Espresso Bar & Cafe in Tottenham. Church Public Inn in Palgrave. Four Corners Bakery or Tom's Family Restaurant in Caledon East.

© OpenStreetMap contributors

Route 35 – Tottenham to Caledon

Scan me

173

Route 36: Forks of the Credit to Erin

Elora Cataract Trailway

Distance: 20.4 km return

Riding Time: 2 hours

Difficulty: Level 1 (All Ages)

Ride Type: Nature-lover, Romantic

Surface: Crushed stone

Facility Type: 100% path

Elevation Gain/Loss: +55m / -60m (southbound)

Max/Min Grade: 5.8%

Starting Point & Parking: Forks of the Credit Provincial Park

Alternate Access Points: Erin Community Centre

Hiking Options: Many side trails to explore at Forks of the Credit

Biking Options: The trailway continues west of Erin to Hillsburgh, Orton, Belwood, Belwood Lake Conservation Area, Fergus and Elora

Connections to Other Routes: Trans Canada Trail

This all ages adventure is a 20 km (return) trip from Forks of the Credit Provincial Park along the Elora Cataract Trailway, which operated as a railway until 1993. It's a pleasant and scenic ride to the Town of Erin. The village centre is about 500 metres to the south of the trail where you'll find plenty of options for lunch or treats, like ice cream from Bailey's Ice Cream or the famous donuts from Holtom's Bakery. You'll see a lot of peaceful contryside as you head back on this flat, crushed stone trail. Those wanting more can continue west of Erin as far as Elora.

174

The Cataract waterfalls lookout at Forks of the Credit as the Credit River drops to the valley floor

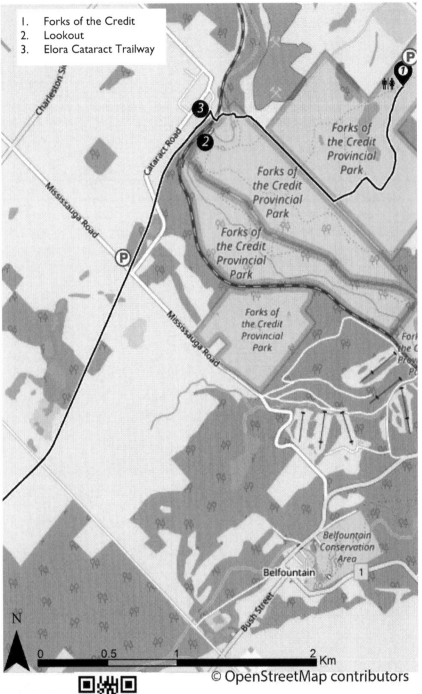

1. Forks of the Credit
2. Lookout
3. Elora Cataract Trailway

Charleston St

Cataract Road

Mississauga Road

Mississauga Road

Forks of the Credit Provincial Park

Forks of the Credit Provincial Park

Forks of the Credit Provincial Park

Forks of the Credit Provincial Park

For the C Prov Pa

Belfountain Conservation Area

Belfountain

N

0   0.5   1   2 Km

© OpenStreetMap contributors

Route 36 –
Forks of the Credit to Erin (1 of 2)

🍴 Holtom's Bakery or Bailey's Ice Cream in Erin

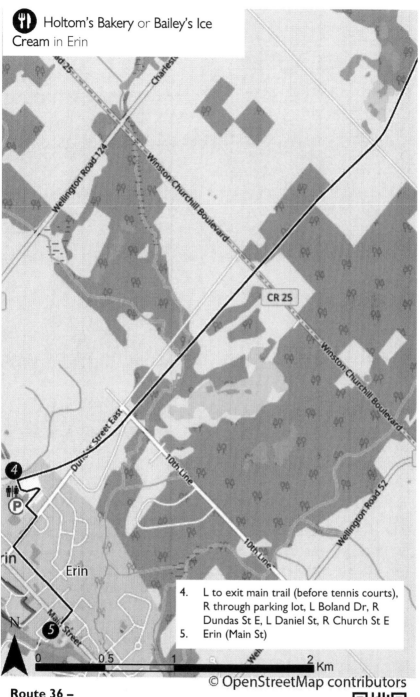

CR 25

4. L to exit main trail (before tennis courts), R through parking lot, L Boland Dr, R Dundas St E, L Daniel St, R Church St E
5. Erin (Main St)

0   0.5   1   2 Km

© OpenStreetMap contributors

Route 36 –
Forks of the Credit to Erin (2 of 2)

Scan me

Route 37: Bronte Creek

Orchard Park to Bronte Creek Provincial Park

Distance: 10.0 km loop

Riding Time: 1 hour

Difficulty: Level 1 (All Ages)

Ride Type: Park-Hopper, Cultural Explorer

Surface: 28% paved, 62% crushed stone

Facility Type: 100% path

Elevation Gain/Loss: +/-65m

Max/Min Grade: 5.2%

Starting Point & Parking: Orchard Community Park in Burlington

Alternate Access Points: Bronte Creek Provincial Park Day Use Parking ($)

Hiking Options: Ravine and loggine trail in the Park is more rugged than the main trail

Biking Options: Trail continues west of Orchard Park

Connections to Other Routes:

Here's an adventure for the whole family. Ride ten kilometres (return) along the Twelve Mile Creek Trail to Bronte Creek Provincial Park, where it's free entry if you arrive by biking or hiking. The park features a 50 metre deep ravine, children's farm with animals, turn-of-the-century farmhouse, disc golf course, nature centre and massive swimming pool to cool off in.

Ice cream bar from the Park Store

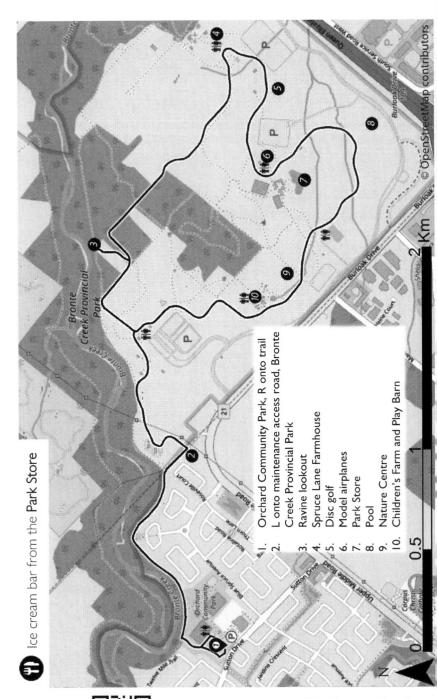

1. Orchard Community Park, R onto trail
2. L onto maintenance access road, Bronte
   Creek Provincial Park
3. Ravine lookout
4. Spruce Lane Farmhouse
5. Disc golf
6. Model airplanes
7. Park Store
8. Pool
9. Nature Centre
10. Children's Farm and Play Barn

© OpenStreetMap contributors

Route 37 – Bronte Creek

Scan me

Route 38:
Hamilton Beach

Spencer Smith Park in
Burlington to
Confederation Park in
Hamilton

Distance: 19.4 km return

Riding Time: 2 hours

Difficulty: Level 1 (All Ages)

Ride Type: Romantic, Park-Hopper

Surface: Paved

Facility Type: 100% path

Elevation Gain/Loss: 0

Max/Min Grade: 0.9%

Starting Point & Parking:
Spencer Smith Park in
Burlington

Alternate Access Points:
Beachway Park, Kinsman Park,
Confederation Park

Hiking Options: 5 km
(return): Confederation Park to
Van Wagner's Beach has
restored beaches and sand
dunes plus some casual eateries
and patios

Biking Options: 15 km
(return): turn around at
Hutch's Restaurant

**Connections to Other
Routes:** HamBur Loop (53
km), Waterfront Trail

The Hamilton Recreation
Beach Trail is completely
off-road and follows the
Lake Ontario shoreline
from Spencer Smith Park
under the Burlington Canal
Lift Bridge to
Confederation Park.
Interpretive panels explain
the history of Hamilton's
waterfront. There are two
wonderful restaurants, a
major waterpark and great
beaches where you can
take a dip in the lake. This
one has some fun stops!

181

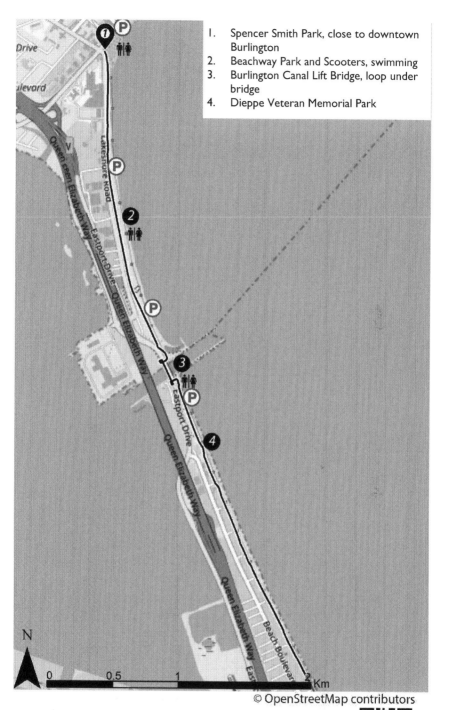

1. Spencer Smith Park, close to downtown Burlington
2. Beachway Park and Scooters, swimming
3. Burlington Canal Lift Bridge, loop under bridge
4. Dieppe Veteran Memorial Park

© OpenStreetMap contributors

Route 38 – Hamilton Beach (1 of 2)

183

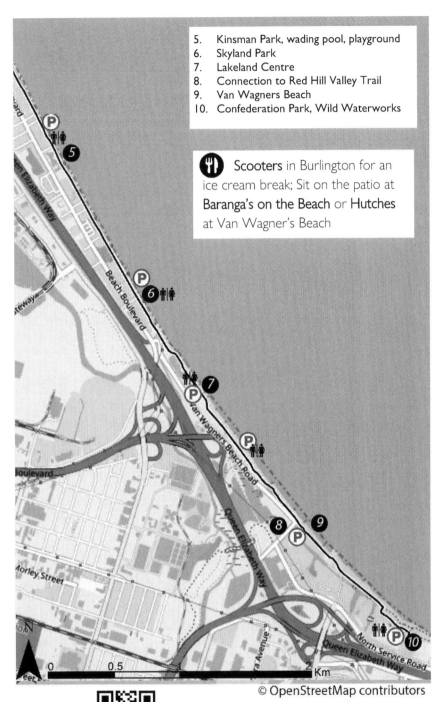

5. Kinsman Park, wading pool, playground
6. Skyland Park
7. Lakeland Centre
8. Connection to Red Hill Valley Trail
9. Van Wagners Beach
10. Confederation Park, Wild Waterworks

Scooters in Burlington for an ice cream break; Sit on the patio at **Baranga's on the Beach** or **Hutches** at Van Wagner's Beach

© OpenStreetMap contributors

Scan me

Route 39: Hamilton Waterfront

Princess Point to Eastpoint Park

Distance: 15.6 km return

Riding Time: 1.5 hours

Difficulty: Level 1 (All Ages)

Ride Type: Nature lover; Cultural Explorer; Romantic

Surface: Paved

Facility Type: 100% path

Elevation Gain/Loss: +32 m / - 33 m (eastbound)

Max/Min Grade: 6.7%

Starting Point & Parking: Princess Point

Alternate Access Points: Bayfront Park, Eastpoint Park

Hiking Options: From Princess Point, there are 18 km of hiking trails in Cootes Paradise Nature Sanctuary with some of the best birding around

Biking Options: Start at Bayfront Park and go either east or west

Connections to Other Routes: HamBur Loop (53 km), Watefront Trail

This 15 km (return) route follows the Desjardin Trail and Waterfront Trail along Hamilton Harbour through some beautiful public spaces along the waterfront and on to a historic naval ship and national historic site. You'll also find cafes, ice cream, and boat cruises nearby. The route starts at Princess Point, a gateway to Cootes Paradise Nature Sanctuary managed by Royal Botanical Gardens. Climb the stairs for an incredible view at the Waterfront Trail lookout. There's lots to explore along this route!

1. Princess Point, Desjardin Recreational Trail
2. York Blvd, lookout point (climb the stairs for the view), Hamilton Harbour Waterfront Trail
3. Bayfront Park
4. Pier 4 Park
5. HMCS Haida
6. Eastwood Park

🍴 Williams Fresh Cafe near the Harbour West Marina; Collective Arts Brewing near Eastwood Park

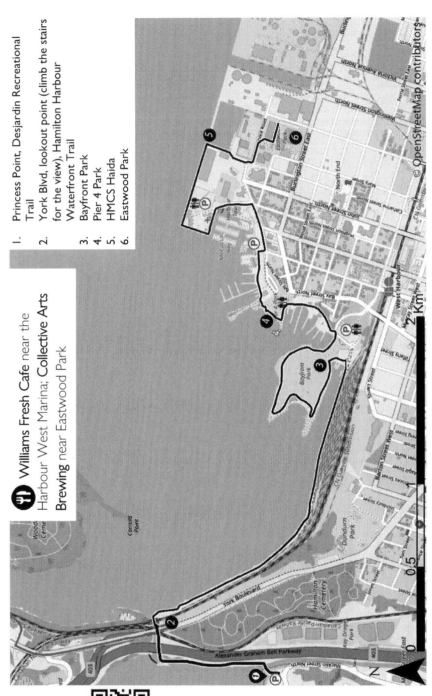

© OpenStreetMap contributors

Route 39 – Hamilton Waterfront

Route 40: Hamilton to Brantford
Rail Trail

Distance: 41.4 km one way, 82.8 km return

Riding Time: 8 hours

Difficulty: Level 3 (Fit)

Ride Type: Nature-lover; Cultural Explorer

Surface: Crushed stone

Facility Type: 98% path, 2% quiet streets

Elevation Gain/Loss: +268 m / -165 m (westbound)

Max/Min Grade: 7.2%

Starting Point & Parking: Parking at the end of Studholme Rd in Hamilton

Alternate Access Points: Dundas Valley Conservation Area, Jerseyville, Brantford Civic Centre

Hiking Options: Dundas Valley Conservation Area trails

Biking Options: 16km (return): turn around at Dundas Trail Centre; for a one-way ride, consider a car shuttle or the bus back from Brantford bus terminal. Or make it a multi-day trip with an overnight in Brantford or Cambridge or a unique farmstay at Heart's Content Organic Farm

The crushed stone trail follows a section of the old Toronto, Hamilton and Buffalo Railway (TH&B) route and offers some of the best biking and hiking opportunities in southern Ontario. Start in Hamilton and follows the scenic Dundas Valley to downtown Brantford and the banks of the Grand River where you'll find a waterpark and casino. Visit the Woodland Cultural Centre to learn about Southern Ontario's First Nations past, present, and future. Leave the buzz of the city and move through this peaceful natural corridor.

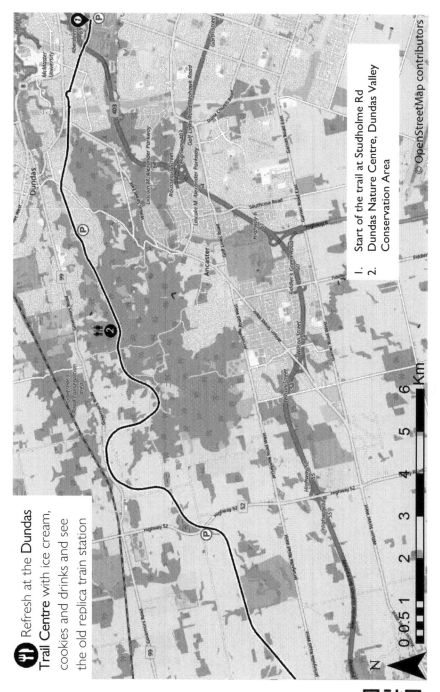

Refresh at the **Dundas Trail Centre** with ice cream, cookies and drinks and see the old replica train station

1. Start of the trail at Studholme Rd
2. Dundas Nature Centre, Dundas Valley Conservation Area

© OpenStreetMap contributors

0 0.5 1   2   3   4   5   6 Km

N

Route 40 – Hamilton to Brantford (1 of 2)

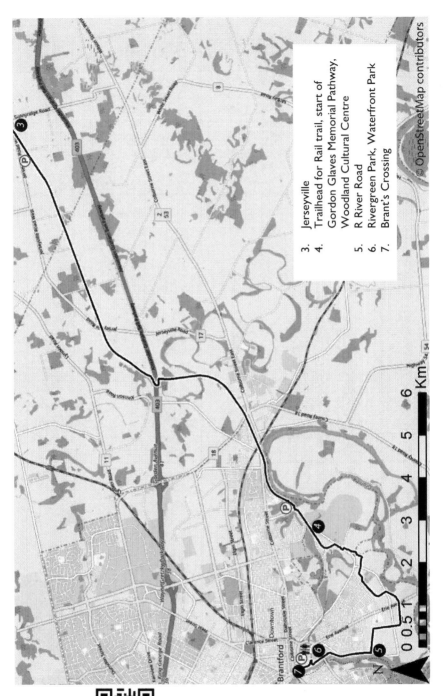

3. Jerseyville
4. Trailhead for Rail trail, start of Gordon Glaves Memorial Pathway, Woodland Cultural Centre
5. R River Road
6. Rivergreen Park, Waterfront Park
7. Brant's Crossing

© OpenStreetMap contributors

Scan me

Route 40 – Hamilton to Brantford (2 of 2)

CHAPTER 8

When women, children, and the elderly, not just aggressive young men, start to see the bike as an easy way to go shopping, to school, or to work, then our cities will start to enjoy improvements in our street life, our economy, our health, and our transportation systems."—Tom Babin, Frostbike

8. EVERYDAY BIKING

When I was a kid, a bicycle took me places. However, by sixteen I traded that freedom for a car. Ten years later, I tried something new—biking to work. The journey was about a twenty minute bike ride each way. Part of the route was along a trail, and it was wonderful. I arrived with a smile across my face, energized and ready to take on the day. I loved the feeling of moving beyond the speed of walking or running, and still on my own power. I didn't realize it right away, but that summer in Thunder Bay, Ontario, I rediscovered my childhood joy for cycling.

I've met some wonderful people who have shared their positive, personal, and inspiring stories about cycling. Max got into the best shape of his life after becoming a year-round bike commuter in his fifties. Lija was able to sell her family's second car and reduce her environmental impact. Shiv, after suffering two heart attacks, turned his health around and built a deeper connection with his son on their daily ride to school. Odette gave up the stress of traffic in her car-centric neighbourhood. My mom, in need of knee replacements, found her mobility once again with a bike. These people and many others have led me to believe that they way we move around our city affects our health and well-being.

Biking my kids to school is a chance to spend quality time outside together. I love seeing their confidence grow. The day my son Noah was finally able to ride to the top of a particular hill, he was so excited to go home and tell his  mom. Getting places by walking or biking is something my kids are proud of. There are still days when they complain, but watching them explore, discover, and wonder about the world around them on their way to school is time well spent.

The unknown can be scary, but it is also a chance to challenge yourself, learn and grow. When was the last time you tried something new? I've realized that we sometimes put ourselves on autopilot. Our habits become ingrained, and we don't think about the best mode for our trip before getting in the car. I encourage you to be an everyday cyclist. Bike to a soccer game. Bike to a friend's house. Bike to the dentist. Bike to the train station. Bike to the coffee shop. Bike to the market. If you travel by bike, you're more likely to arrive with a smile, you'll feel better and you'll have seen much more along the way.

Shawn's Top 10 Tips
for More Enjoyable Biking

Here are a few things I've learned along the way that will help make for a safer and more joyful ride:

1. **The sweet spot is two to five kilometres**. Try biking this distance to your local library, the store, a friend's house or the GO Transit Station. It's quick, reliable, fun and satisfying.

2. **Get a tune up**. Bike shops often have special deals during their slower winter months. Get a professional mechanic to give your bike some love. Small things like adjusting your gears or brakes can make a big difference. Are you hearing crickets? For a quieter ride, add some bike lube to your chain and wipe away the excess. Your chain will last longer and shift gears better too.

3. **Be cautious with sidewalk riding**. If you ride on the sidewalk because the road is just too busy and there aren't many pedestrians, ride in the same direction as traffic flow, and treat every driveway like an intersection. Be courteous and go on the grass to pass anyone on foot. As you gain confidence, you'll find the road is usually the best place to ride, especially on quiet streets.

4. **Wear a helmet**. It can lessen the severity of a brain injury if you happen to hit your head, and also models good behaviour for kids. They come in stylish designs now too.

5. **Add some fun, colourful wheel lights** to the standard front and rear set to help you be seen at night. It will get many smiles from the people you pass.

6. **Add a wireless bluetooth speaker** to your bike. Cruising around to your favourite tunes is so much fun. Be sure not to use headphones so you can stay aware of your surroundings.

7. **Pump up those tires**. Riding with underinflated tires is harder work, and you are more likely to get a flat.

8. **Equip your bike with a front or rear rack** so you can carry some cargo. It comes in really handy and you'll impress people as you ride by with the greatest of ease carrying a basket full of groceries.

9. **Go electric.** Pedal-assisted e-bikes combine a fairly conventional bike with a battery and motor that helps out when you're pedalling to make it easier to get up hills, accelerate away from lights and cruise along. The extra boost means you can ride extra distance more easily. E-bikes are both practical and exhiliarating. Try one at your local bike shop.

10. **Find some people to ride with**. Cycling can be a wonderful social activity. Share your rides through mobile apps and social media and stay motivated. Is there a bike club in your community or workplace? Are there local events happening? Get involved. Your city needs you!

Overcoming Barriers to Biking

"It's for the young and fit"

Riding a bike is not just for the spandex-wearing crowd. It's for just about everyone regardless of their fitness level. People can go further on a bike than walking or jogging and it's low impact. Plus, the more they do it, the easier it gets. For many people, bicycling continues right into their 80's and beyond, and the advent of a new generation of power-assist bicycles and tricycles makes riding into old age easier than ever before.

Not everyone learns to ride a bike when they're young. They may have had limited access to a bike or were involved in other activities instead. People of all ages can learn to ride a bike in just a few hours with some practice and help from a more experienced rider. For seniors, the increasing use of electric-assist bikes and trikes means that physical strength is less of a barrier. For those with mobility needs, adaptive cycles like a hand-powered trike may make trips easier than walking. Cycling gives people more transportation options and independence, regardless of age. Add this fun, healthy activity to the many things that you can do.

"It takes too long, or it's too far"

In urban areas, travel speeds are comparable to a bicycle. Add in peak period traffic congestion, and a trip by bicycle can be the fastest, most reliable, and most convenient way for short trips. In Ontario, about half of all trips are less than five kilometres (three miles), which can easily be done by bike in under 20 minutes by an average person on a bike. For longer trips, combine biking with transit and get to and from the station or stop more quickly. Biking to your destination does take extra planning, but once you get the hang of it, it becomes routine.

Studies have shown that people who don't walk or bike dramatically overestimate how long it would take to get to a destination, especially when the trips are short.

Challenge #1: Time how long it takes you to get to a destination you go to frequently (such as your church, a grocery store, or your kids' school) but make sure you track it door-to-door. That means accounting for time finding a parking spot, parking, and walking to the door. Then try biking that trip the next time you have to make it, and compare the times.

"I'll get too sweaty"

In North America, cycling has often been thought of as a sport for spandex-clad road riders. While we tend to associate cycling with drop handlebars and high speeds, the reality is that in most countries, cycling is often a relaxed mode of transport in which the top speed is not important. Go as fast or as slow as you want. If you bike at a leisurely pace, there is no more sweating than moderate walking for the same amount of time. If you want to go fast, e-bikes offer a pedal-assist option that can zoom you up hills without breaking a sweat. Or, you can ride a regular bike at a vigorous pace, reap the health benefits, and freshen up at your final destination.

Challenge #2: Try biking to work, or combining biking and transit like biking to a GO Station. Maybe there's someone at your workplace that already does it and can help get you started?

"It's too tiring"

Riding a bicycle is energizing. When you reach a certain point in a ride, the physical activity causes your brain to release good chemicals into your bloodstream, and you feel fantastic. Nothing beats a daily dose of athletically-induced endorphins to lift your spirit and your energy level. You won't get that by sitting in a car!

"It's not safe"

This is common perception, but research shows that cycling is no more dangerous than car travel or walking. Choosing routes along quiet streets or with bicycle infrastructure like protected bike lanes makes it even safer. There are also some safety rules and tips that you can familiarise yourself with to minimize the risks, such as avoiding distractions, being aware of your surroundings, and positioning yourself to stay visible. Across North America, a complete streets approach is beginning to take hold and we are seeing more bike protected bike lanes and lower traffic speeds, which improves safety for everyone.

Research on life expectancy shows that bicycle commuters live longer than car commuters because of the regular exercise. One study showed that those who exercise for an average of 15 minutes a day live an average of three years longer. If you do the math, that means that for every one minute of bicycling, you can expect an extra three minutes added to your lifespan. Cool!

"It's not practical for carrying loads"

A practical bike for commuting will have a rear rack or front carrier which can carry a considerable load. A cargo bike, trailer, or carrier option make shopping by bike an easy activity. A bike doesn't have to be used for every trip, but it is an option. There are some who even pick up their Christmas tree by bike.

Challenge #3: Equip your bike with a way to carry cargo, and go shopping by bike. Compare it with the experience by car.

"It means breathing in polluted air"

While air pollution in major cities is of increasing concern, research has shown that the benefits of bicycling greatly outweigh the effects of polluted air. Studies also show that the air quality inside motor vehicles is worse than outside. Physical inactivity is the much bigger public health issue. Still, there are a range of measures cyclists can take to limit their exposure, from taking quieter back routes, to cycling at particular times of the day.

"It's not practical with children"

There are practical ways for you to bring young children along with you by bike in a fast and safe way. Trailers, child seats, tag alongs, and cargo bikes are all excellent options to travel together as a family. Once they are old enough, most children appreciate the freedom that a bicycle gives. The reason many people believe it is too difficult to ride somewhere with children is because there are not safe places to do so: off-road paths, protected bike lanes, or quiet residential streets. Look at a cycling map to plan your next trip. You'll find that there are many great routes in the City and bike network improvements are being made each year.

Challenge #4: If you have young children, take them to school by bicycle. If you live too far, drive and park a few blocks from the school and walk the rest of the way together. What do your kids prefer?

"The weather isn't right"

For most places including Ontario, cycling is practical for short trips most of the time. Out of the 365 days each year, it's likely that 350 can be considered good biking days. The other 15 days are probably not good for going out at all, regardless of travel mode. In cities where there is good snow clearing, people can continue to ride bikes year round. For example, at a school of 1200 students in Oulu, Finland, about 1000 students bike to school through the winter. There, it is the norm. The Finnish say in jest that there are no bad weather days for cycling, only a poor choice in clothing.

Challenge #5: Try biking in winter. Pick a sunny day with bare pavement and a route along quiet streets. Was it what you expected?

Connecting Online

Here are some ways that you can share your experiences, stay motivated and connect with others:

 I'd love your feedback about the trails, their conditions and your experiences. What did you like most and least? Do you have any tips for other cyclists and hikers of the routes? You can post comments in the Resources section of the website. happybiketrails.com/resources

 Did you complete a challenge? Email your stories. I'd love to hear from you!
shawn@happybiketrails.com

 Share photos and videos on social media with the hashtag **#happybiketrails** or tag **@happybiketrails** on Instagram, Twitter, and Facebook

Bikemonth.ca: Bike Month is a celebration of cycling across the Greater Toronto and Hamilton Area. It starts at the end of May with Bike to Work Day and Bike to School Week and continues through the month of June. There are many ways to participate, from charity rides, guided tours, festivals, workshops, races and more. Pledge to ride for a chance to win some great prizes.

Multi-Day Adventures

Here are some longer adventures that expand on some of the routes in this book. Add these to your bucket list! Find more information at the following links.

Great Lakes Waterfront Trail
Routes 2, 3, 4, 13, 14, 27, 28, 29, 32, 38, 39 waterfronttrail.org

PanAm Path
Routes 2, 3, 5, 8, 12, 13, 14, 15, 16, 17, 18 panampath.org

The Great Trail (Trans Canada Trail)
Routes 2, 3, 4, 5, 8, 12, 13, 14, 27, 28, 29, 30, 31, 32, 33, 35, 36, 39, 40 thegreattrail.ca

Toronto Circle Loop (86 km)
Routes 2, 3, 5, 9, 10, 11, 15, 16, 19
ridewithgps.com/ambassador_routes/1551-toronto-trails-ravines-june-tour-updated

Lake to Lake Cycling Route and Walking Trail (120 km)
Routes 4, 5, 9, 10, 22, 23, 25, 26 york.ca/laketolake

Getting Involved

Here are some organizations that are helping to create better biking and hiking experiences. Learn more at the links provided.

Ontario By Bike

The Ontario By Bike™ Network is a program certifying and promoting bicycle friendly businesses and cycle tourism across Ontario. The Network is open to accommodations, food services, attractions, cycling related businesses and organizations interested in cycle tourism. For cyclists, the Ontario By Bike™ Network offers a variety of information on cycling in Ontario, inspiring visitors and residents to explore more by bike. Find the bike-friendly businesses near you. ontariobybike.ca

Waterfront Regeneration Trust

The Waterfront Regeneration Trust is a registered charity committed to connecting people to their Great Lakes. They do this through work to complete, enhance and promote the Waterfront Trail. Today the Trail is 3000 km along Lake Erie, Lake Ontario and the St. Lawrence River. It connects 140 communities and natural areas, beaches, wetlands, historic sites. It is both a celebration of our Great Lakes heritage and a commitment to regenerating our waterfront. waterfronttrail.org

Share the Road Cycling Coalition

The Share the Road Cycling Coalition is a provincial cycling advocacy organization working to build a bicycle-friendly Ontario. They work in partnership with municipal, provincial and federal governments, the business community, road safety organizations and other non-profits to enhance access for bicyclists on roads and trails, improve safety for all bicyclists, and educate citizens on the value and importance of safe bicycling for healthy lifestyles and healthy communities. sharetheroad.ca

Cycle Toronto

 Cycle Toronto is a member-supported not-for-profit organization that works to make Toronto a healthy, safe and vibrant cycling city for all. They are focused on advocacy, education and encouragement, and work to shape policy and infrastructure, and build community to transform the city's cycling culture. They engage a diversity of people in our work, pursuing evidence-based solutions that make cycling a viable option for all Torontonians. cycleto.ca

Toronto Bicycling Network

 Toronto Bicycling Network is Toronto's largest recreational cycling club, rated the City's #1 cycling club by BlogTO and Readers Choice. TBN offers rides throughout the week and on weekends as well as affordable trips outside Toronto and a wide range of winter activities. tbn.ca

The Centre for Active Transportation

 The Centre for Active Transportation (TCAT) has a vision of vibrant cities with clean air, a healthy population, and a transportation system that prioritizes walking and cycling. Its mission is to advance knowledge and evidence to build support for safe and inclusive streets for walking and cycling. They believe that active transportation plays a critical role in creating environmentally and economically sustainable cities. tcat.ca

Toronto and Region Conservation Authority

 Toronto and Region Conservation Authority (TRCA) works with municipalities and other partners to look after the watersheds of the Toronto region and its Lake Ontario waterfront. TRCA has developed The Trail Strategy for the Greater Toronto Region as a call to action to renew our collective efforts to complete, expand and manage the Greater Toronto Region Trail Network with the next generation of trails. trca.ca/conservation/greenspace-management/trail-strategy

Photo Credits
All photos used with permission; *=Instagram

Page

3. © [kamaga] / Adobe Stock
7. Shawn Smith
12. Marlaine Koehler
13. Images Ontario
14. Shawn Smith
15. Images Ontario, Shawn Smith
16. Shawn Smith
19. Images Ontario
20. Shawn Smith
21. Images Ontario, Vernon Raineil / Unsplash
22. © [wild_wind] / Adobe Stock
23. © [pahis] / Adobe Stock
24. © [spotmatikphoto] / Adobe Stock
26. © [Robert Philip] / Adobe Stock
28. CAASCO; Cycle Toronto
29. Shawn Smith
30. Cycle Toronto
31. Shawn Smith
32. Shawn Smith, Shawn Smith
34. Images Ontario
36. Irin4kononenko*
38. Images Ontario, chandu_144*, christyzhong*, naseem_m*
39. Lindsay Swanson*, Shawn Smith, suzlee72*, inconspicuous_account*
40. Bob Whalen*
41. riptide338*, g_theathletelife*, Shawn Smith, Shawn Smith, Bob Whalen*, Joey Schwartz, Joey Schwartz, leescottwowpowerwalking*
44. Images Ontario
45. Grace Ko*, sandarroch*, Inya Ivkovic*, Dan Springer*
46. brendanschnurr*, redrovertoronto*, Shawn Smith
49. sims.pix*
50. Michael Monastyrskyj*, Caroline Mercer*, ollievons*, dogville808*, sukizann*, Vanessa Shah*
51. wanderjoyously*, homesweetkaryn*, Ariel Fried, madmal99*, pedaltoronto*
54. pdalt*
55. Robyn Short*, shawkels*, Shawn Smith, Brian Chan*, Shawn Smith

58. Grainne Brophy*
59. Michael Desbiens*, Heirloom Toronto*, gowithjon*, engclan*, brashhhh*
62. Alex Wong*
63. Catharine Mackenzie*, Catharine Mackenzie*, Mark Junop*, running_thru_nature*, Norman Valdez*
66. christophefriedli*
67. Molly Donovan*, Harvey Cooper*, Christina Nolan*, toronto_sean*, Krysha Littlewood*
69. nermintekes*
70. Pabby88*, Shawn Smith, Larry J Herscovitch*, Jim Chartier*, Jayalakshmi Dinesh*
72. Shawn Smith
73. Shawn Smith
76. Sreeraj Balagovindan*
77. Shawn Smith
79. mimisugs*
80. Jennifer Wilson Campbell*, Shawn Smith, pat3sha_p*, Catharine Mackenzie*, Shawn Smith
82. sreeraj_ravi*,
83. Jenny Foster Vaya, weekenderer*, pixinthesix*, *_charles.harvey_*
86. claidy_photo*
87. daydreamer88*, annmarievrscaj*, Grace Ko*, jagienka9*, 3p_sarf*
90. a.m. guerrero*
91. Michael Mitchener*, Heather Jackson, theasumo*, Sophie Boucaut*, Michelle Karunaratne*
93. lisabalestri*
94. Heather Jackson, Heather Jackson, Sara Maginn Pacella*, Jean Trivett*, Heather Jackson
97. phantheman2
98. Heather Jackson, priya.ramsingh*, Heather Jackson, Heather Jackson, Heather Jackson
100. Samad Shirazie*
101. Heather Jackson, Lisa Salazar*, Shawn Smith, Shawn Smith, Shawn Smith
103. mohammadnazarill*
104. Shawn Smith, Mark Joven Alcabedos*, Shawn Smith, Shawn Smith, shezzym*

106. neekbreek*
107. mohitrajadhyakesha*, Fresh City Farm Downsview, Shawn Smith, Shawn Smith, Shawn Smith
110. Shawn Smith
111. Shawn Smith
112. Shawn Smith, Michelle Hannikainen*, pitriephotography*, Shawn Smith, sw33tqt*
114. Shawn Smith
115. Shawn Smith
117. Shawn Smith
118. Shawn Smith, Shawn Smith, Shawn Smith, peterbarmstrong*, Shawn Smith
119. Shawn Smith
122. Shawn Smith
123. Shawn Smith
126. Shawn Smith
127. Shawn Smith
128. Dave McLaughlin, Shawn Smith, Shawn Smith, Shawn Smith, Shawn Smith
132. Shawn Smith
133. Shawn Smith
134. Shawn Smith
138. Shawn Smith
139. thusiakak*, Shawn Smith, Shawn Smith, Shawn Smith, Shawn Smith, Shawn Smith
142. Justin Jones
143. Pav-Harry Fregillana*, Shawn Smith, jeep_hair*, photopixbytina*, Charles Smith*
145. cyclinktheworld*
146. Mike Drake*, smittenmitten22*, Peter Cameron*, chloejuleann*
150. 99pennylane*
151. Bill McCollom*, Joe Pantalleresco*, 99pennylane*, thatadrianm*
153. jannarf*
154. Dorothy Kowpak, Dorothy Kowpak, Winnie Lai, Dorothy Kowpak, Dorothy Kowpak
156. Shawn Smith, Rudy Limeback
158. Christina Somers / getoutside.today (www.getoutsidetoday.ca)

159. nobodypannix*, Jane Chapman*, Tracey Finlay, randys_travels*, chizzayon*
162. Katharine Kurniawan*
163. Dave McLaughlin, Jason Harrell*, oregon_runner*, Sarah Crook*, sunshine_runner*
166. Shawn Smith
167. Shawn Smith, Shawn Smith, mirmir3000*, Harsharan Singh
170. Shawn Smith
171. and_into_the_forest_i___go*, Shawn Smith, Shawn Smith, Monika Stepien*, Mark Muzzin*
172. Shawn Smith, HTDesigns.ca*, Shawn Smith, Shawn Smith, Shawn Smith
174. Brian Travis*
175. blitzthewonderdog*, © 2018, Michael James Perry*, Mike von Massow / mikevonmassow*, Mia Di Sotto Villella*
178. _leena.hk*
179. Amanda Hollingworth*, Shah Het, Chazz Balkwill*, Chazz Balkwill*
181. Anuja Vaibhav*
182. heyitsticzer*, epikism*, Ivan Arredondo*, Laurie Simnett*, Anna Olech*
185. Vikram Hardatt
186. lisa.hikes*, Mitchell Theriault*, itsmejo_c*, John Fraser*, alifelikethis*
187. inhabitingtrees*, cass.o.frass*, Sue Abell*, moveablefeastblog*, Jeff Rodrigue
189. Dorothy Kowpak
190. Brian Warring*, brodydendekker*, Dorothy Kowpak, Katie Halsall*, Matt Cassell*
193. © [Christian Müller] / Adobe Stock
194. Shawn Smith
196. Shawn Smith, Shawn Smith, Justin Jones
197. © [pikselstock] / Adobe Stock
198. Shawn Smith
199. © [edbockstock] / Adobe Stock
200. © [gorosi] / Adobe Stock
201. Shawn Smith
202. © [piksel stock] / Adobe Stock
203. Ontario Images
204. Ontario Images

Made in the USA
Coppell, TX
11 October 2021